Forces For Freedom

Forces For Freedom

by
ROBERT STANTON

IN COLLABORATION WITH
ARTHUR FITZ-RICHARD

Public Affairs Press, Washington, D. C.

TO ROTARIANS EVERYWHERE
AND
TO THE HARRY CAMP ENDOWMENT
AT STANFORD UNIVERSITY

FOREWORD

It is a pleasure to commend this book to the attention of all who are concerned to preserve individual liberty and enhance human dignity.

Mr. Stanton makes no pretentious claims for his work. As a businessman with international interests and as an occasional public servant he has observed and reflected upon the public affairs of his times. His reflections have persuaded him that the enterprise and freedom of the individual have been and are in serious danger of being impaired, even thwarted. His reminiscences reveal why he thinks so.

The recent debates as to "The National Purpose" has produced clarion calls for more vigorous and informed leadership and for deeper individual commitment. Mr. Stanton issues the same sort of summons.

Freedom in and of itself is not an active agent. It exists only in the hearts and minds of individual men and women. They alone hold it in their power to preserve freedom or to lose it. Mr. Stanton's reflections remind us of that fact. The reminder is timely. Each of us should make it insistent.

J. E. WALLACE STERLING
President, Stanford University

PREFACE

So much has been written and said about the Communist menace in a general way, a great many persons, who should be alert to the danger, have become inured instead, and have assumed an attitude, bordering on apathy, when someone suggests that our American way of life is threatened. Looking about them, they see no semblance of Communist party activity in our midst, no men of importance making approving speeches, no newspapers or magazines advocating the system and, in fact, no soap box oratory in any of our large cities. Does this mean that we are safe and secure and that complacency is justifiable? I don't think so.

My purpose in writing a book on the subject is to focus attention on the stark reality of Communist aggression affecting our economy and ultimate freedom. I have tried to do this by demonstrating specifically how easily Communism can infect our society, and may be doing so. My conclusions are based upon a life-long experience in the production and distribution of goods and services, and some contact with a totalitarian regime. Communism is not introduced with fan-fare and the clash of arms. It arrives stealthily, unheard and unseen. It works quietly in the minds of men, eventually manifesting its presence in strange happenings all over the land. Labor disputes take on overtones of Marxist doctrine, racial and religious bigotry flare up in unexpected places, patriotism weakens and men seeking election to public office find that grandiose promises of unsound fiscal and economic benefits produce the winning votes.

Why is the man-in-the-street, so-called, oblivious to Communistic infiltration? Is he envious? Greedy? Self-centered? Ignorant? The American man-in-the-street is none of these. The truth is he is simply too sophisticated to become aroused by philosophic speculation about the trend of affairs. He accepts our hard won and precious freedom as nonchalantly as he does all the natural and man-made resources America possesses. He assumes our way of life can and will go on forever. This attitude, more than any other consideration, impelled me to undertake the writing of a book at this time of my life.

My hope is that readers of the facts I am presenting will bestir themselves, and help to stamp out the little fires of false propaganda before they develop into a conflagration. Soviet Communism is

7

forty-three years old. The system has grown and expanded, due to
the efforts of dedicated and ruthless adherents and the blindness of
some ultimate victims. Thirty years ago one of the prominent and
influential Kremlin leaders, Dimitri Z. Manuilsky, said the following:

"War to the hilt between Communism and Capitalism is inevitable. Today, of course, we are not strong enough to attack. Our
time will come in twenty or thirty years. To win we shall need the
element of surprise. The bourgeois will have to be put to sleep. So
we shall begin by launching the most spectacular peace movement on
record. There will be electrifying overtures and unheard of conces-
sions. The Capitalistic countries, stupid and decadent, will rejoice
to cooperate in their own destruction. They will leap at another
chance to be friends. As soon as their guard is down, we shall smash
them with our clenched fists."

No amelioration of this diabolical outline of attack has come
through the years. To the contrary, it is now apparent to all mankind that Soviet leaders are intensifying their drive towards world
domination.

*   *   *

To George Stevens and Michael Dowley I am deeply indebted
for encouragement and advice. Moreover, I owe much to the sponsors
of the Harry Camp Endowment: E. C. Lipman, Edward W. Carter,
Frank W. Folsom, William Lister Rogers, Fred Lazarus, Jr., and
Charles Hobbs.

ROBERT STANTON

San Francisco

CONTENTS

"We need to remember that a concept of the dignity and worth of the individual is perhaps the most significant contribution of American Civilization to human progress and to rededicate ourselves to the difficult realization of the ideal throughout the world."—*Ex-President Herbert C. Hoover.*

"If we are to reanimate the cause of freedom we must be willing to go behind them, to come to grips with forces that have been driving us in a direction contrary to our will."—*Russell Davenport* in *"The Dignity of Man".*

"All are aware Articles of Constitution can remain dead letters. What gives them life is when people themselves live and act according to those principles embodied in their Constitution."—*Chancellor Adenauer.*

"The great principles we have inherited from the world's experience are not statements to be read occasionally. They are actual forces to be directed upon whatever we do every day at our job. We work with the forces. But they work for us."—*J. C. Penney.*

"The ideal of freedom is a powerful, solid and political realism—an Ideal stronger now than ever. Only those people who can choose their destiny are able to maintain human rights."—*General Charles DeGaulle.*

"We voice our hope and our belief that we can help to heal this divided world. Thus may the weight of fear and the weight of arms be taken from the burdened shoulders of mankind—may the light of freedom coming to all darkened lands flame brightly—until at last the darkness is no more."—*Dwight D. Eisenhower at his second inaugural.*

I

FREEDOM IS MY BUSINESS

Of all peoples on the face of this earth, Americans are the most blessed with freedom. That I happened to be born in free America, is to me the greatest piece of luck ever to come my way. From my observation, most Americans are not so appreciative of their birthright—they tend to look on freedom as a natural possession, rather like their baby hair, which though it may vanish, is all the time being replaced by a sturdier growth. They take freedom for granted, and when confronted by evidence that other nations are not so fortunate, they react in astonishment, as if to say: All people have hair, why are all people not free?

If I may claim to any distinction, it must be in my role as a life-long witness of the ways of freedom, its achievements and its loss.

I was a child when my foreign-born grandfather impressed upon me that free America was a miracle in a world of oppression. He instilled in me a feeling that has stayed with me ever since, a sense of privilege that freedom was mine without a battle.

In the first World War, I witnessed the winning of freedom by European peoples who had not known it for centuries. I had the searing experience of seeing some of the same peoples, in Germany and Czechoslovakia specifically, lose their freedom prior to Word War II. Some of them knew what they were losing, and these truly grieved. Others had to learn they had become prisoners; when they did, grief was no less acute.

I have seen freedoms eroded even here in America, of more recent years; I was an actor in a World War II drama, under the aegis of a national agency, which might have cost us more freedom than any imagine.

I have lived through one of the most remarkable periods of world history, from before the turn of the century until now. I have seen a good deal of the geography of this peculiar globe. I have known many influential people, some of considerable power, and I have learned from them. There may be something of value for other Americans in what I have learned, what I think and feel about our world and our country's place in it.

A great deal has been written to the effect that all peoples are at a fateful crossroads in the decade beginning with 1960, and this, it seems to me, is the truth. As I sit talking in my garden at Atherton, California, two world leaders—the President of the United States and the Premier of Soviet Russia—hold in their hands the power to determine the future of humanity.

Is this not an appalling thing? That the entire human race has become dependent on decisions made by two mortal men? However capably they may be advised, however good their intentions, this is too great a a concentration of power. What is worse, we have reason to doubt the good intent of the Soviet leader. But we have been maneuvered into departing from careful traditional diplomacy—by our friends as well as the enemy. For good or ill, we are committed to these perilous negotiations.

It is a situation especially galling to Americans. With our democratic processes, we have achieved a measure of well-being that is the world's envy. Now we live in danger of having our many material possessions, and the freedoms we enjoy, taken from us. We could lose them, you know, despite the fact that I have as yet to meet many Americans who really believe it.

We can lose our freedoms just as easily through our own shortcomings as through the world conflict between International Communism and the Western Democracies of which everyone is so conscious.

It is felt by much of the rest of the world that we Americans, the most powerful people on earth, a country thrust into a decisive role without wishing it, don't know what we want or where we're going.

Is this true? Far from it. We may be a little confused—but we are not alone in our confusion. Indeed, my feeling is that our opponents are more essentially confused than we, even though fanatic belief in their ideology lends them a formidable strength. In the swiftly changing balances of world affairs we may not always know exactly where to place our weight. But there is no question about our firm resolve to retain our freedoms, or our wish to see other peoples achieve freedoms they may desire, along with an equal level of prosperity.

A basic difficulty is that our intent, our beliefs, have not often been clearly stated to the rest of the world. We have seldom stated them clearly to ourselves.

It *is* true that the average American does not fully appreciate the position our country occupies in the world, nor understand many of the conflicting forces at work in our own system. Some highly placed individuals feel that ordinary people haven't the capacity to grasp the basics of big issues. With this I don't agree at all. The issues have not been made plain enough, nor have the more important of them often been presented in relationship with each other.

Thus there is a need, I feel, for a brief and lucid book that sizes things up generally, and might serve as a ready reference a person can use to keep track of fundamentals in all the wheeling and dealing that will be going on in this sorry world over the next years. The present volume is an attempt at writing it.

I do not pretend my effort is highly original. In part it is a distillation of facts and opinion set down in many forms by many other writers. It does, however, tell what a rather ordinary man thinks and feels about it all, in the hope that others may profit. It will try to summarize the problems Americans face today, giving something of background, something of what the future may be like.

This, admittedly, is quite a large order. And you may well ask: who is this fellow Stanton?

A man is made of memories, especially as he gets a bit older, and you may best come to know me by sharing some of mine. A memory I often recall with wonder is that of the world I knew in my turn-of-the-century adolescence.

I saw quite a lot of it, for a boy—New York and Europe as well as San Francisco, which was my birthplace. It was a pleasantly secure world. When I traveled with my father, a glove importer who owned a factory in Germany with my uncle, no passports were required. People everywhere prided themselves on being civilized. A world court sat at The Hague in Holland to settle quarrels among nations. The idea that anything like a world war could happen was preposterous.

After two years at school in Switzerland I returned to San Francisco in time for the great earthquake and fire of 1906. Our house, high on a hill, escaped damage. Aside from the fright and thrill with which I beheld the shaking, blazing city, the outstanding figure of this memory is that of Enrico Caruso. Dazed by a narrow escape from his hotel, the famous tenor climbed the hill alone, pushing a baby carriage containing all he had salvaged of his possessions. To our delight, he remained our guest for several days.

I well remember Stanford University in the years 1907-1910. The natural surroundings charmed me but the curriculum did not. My older brother Arthur kept me there restlessly until he graduated; then I too left, trying a multitude of jobs, delivering groceries and doing other things. Our disgusted father, who had heard me speak in favor of the Workmen's Compensation Act, considered me a Socialist. Perhaps I was a little rebellious.

The threat of war sobered me somewhat, and the United States Army finished the job. During my months at the first officers' training camp at Del Monte, I was forced to work steadily and hard. During this period there came the Preparedness Day parade down Market Street in San Francisco, with the hurling of the I.W.W. bomb by or with the aid of the anarchist Tom Mooney. The explosion missed me by less than fifty yards. I have had little sympathy with anarchists since.

Service in the Signal Corps took me to Kelly Field in Texas — thousands of tents in a sea of mud. Developing a sore throat and receiving orders to the hospital, I faced a decision of some gravity. If a man let himself be hospitalized just then, he'd be bound to catch the flu, and if he caught flu he was the same as dead. I volunteered for shipment overseas as an adjutant. I reached France, but fifteen miles out of Bordeaux I thought I'd never make it.

Our convoy had run into a U-boat wolf pack. Torpedo wakes seemed to be cutting the sea's surface everywhere as sub chasers swarmed to meet us. My ship carried 1,000 colored troops, and the CO feared they might mutiny out of sheer terror. But those colored boys in their life jackets spent their time shooting craps on one side of the deck, and praying on the other, the gamblers occasionally crossing to the praying side, the prayerful often joining the kneeling circles of players. There was no fear, no panic. It crossed my mind that these were free men, free to behave naturally.

Certainly Stanton, armed with a pistol, and with orders to shoot to kill at the first sign of mutiny, never felt more foolish—or more like praying—in his life.

I spent the next two years in France. Undoubtedly the highlight of my Army career occurred when I chanced to locate 100,000 yards of parachute silk in the warehouse of a Paris firm with which Stantons had done business, and bought it for the U.S. Government. I was again lucky in obtaining use of a parachute patent—the enthusiastic inventor invited me to test his gear by jumping off a three-story building, but the 'chute had already been tested in combat and I felt that was enough. Thereafter many more of our fliers survived being shot down.

This is not to imply the French were withholding the silk. They didn't know about it any more than I did until I ran into my father's merchandising friend. As for parachutes, there were never enough either for our allies or ourselves.

War's end found me in Intelligence, researching the results of aerial bombing. In the light of the tremendous strides made since in that branch of military science, my findings were anything but sensational. Few World War I bombers succeeded in scoring really damaging hits. Times have indeed changed.

The family glove factory in Germany had been lost to us, naturally, during the war years. Used to produce military supplies, it had been practically ruined. But several hundred families in the little town of Johanngeorgenstadt were in dire need of the livelihood it had always afforded them. My brothers Arthur and Irwin, both just out of the Army also, agreed that the situation offered opportunity for everybody concerned.

Recovering the property, we formed a new corporation with what capital we could scrape together—and everybody went to work. Soon we found that our employees were suffering for lack of decent housing. By the time we had put up apartment buildings for them, the Stantons were in so deep that success was absolutely imperative. We managed it. After a couple of critical years, the American market began to absorb all the ladies' fine gloves the plant could turn out.

There were still difficulties. Inflation seized Germany by the throat in the 1920's. At its height, simple necessities cost millions of marks, and people carried money in suitcases. My young wife, Lilian, witnessed a tragic episode on a train one day.

A farmer had traveled a few hours to Nuremburg to buy a bull for his herd. Between the time he left home and the time he arrived the money market had run wild, and he discovered the bushel of cash he carried was almost worthless. On his return journey he attempted to jump off the train and kill himself as it sped over a bridge.

The chaotic last years of the well-intended but bumbling Weimar Republic completely demoralized the German people. They had no security whatsoever. The ranks of labor boiled with unrest. Communists made the most of it, fomenting riots and strikes. Hatred of capital became intense. Even in Johann, where most of the workers were relatively well off, we had trouble. On one visit (at this time my work kept me in the States more than abroad) I tore down several posters showing Arthur with his foot on a workman's neck.

A weary nation finally turned to that man of calamitous destiny, Hitler. Or, more accurately, the German people in apathy surrendered to him. It is my opinion that the vast majority detested Nazism, but Hitler promised them stability and their place in the sun—at the price of their freedom.

In 1939, Hitler marched into Czechoslovakia, and we were finished. Shortly afterwards, World War II began.

I am now on the threshold of what I consider to be my most important and illuminating experience — my war-time service in this country as an unsalaried executive of the Office of Price Administration.

My three years with this agency were, without question, the most frustrating of my entire life. I went into the O.P.A. because I felt it my duty. I am a Rotarian and believe in service not only as a member of Rotary but as an individual, and what else was there for me to do when I was asked? The instances of selfless service by members of Rotary Clubs are endless. So I fell into line.

The Emergency Price Control Act granted to its Administrator powers without precedent in the history of this country. It was necessary. Though it introduced into a free economy a system of artificial curbs which would have been intolerable in any time other than one of dire need, without such curbs we could have lost the war on the home front through runaway inflation, crippling our capacity to produce the materials of war needed to win the big battle.

Hastily enacted, the Act had faults, the most serious being the authority delegated to the O.P.A. by Congress to govern almost every facet of our economic life by decree. We were fortunate in obtaining the services of men of ability and integrity throughout the top echelons of the agency. But they had the task of organizing and administering a vast organization which had to be created practically overnight; much of their authority had to be delegated to lesser men.

Therein lay the rub. Too many of the minor administrators simply weren't up to their jobs. Or worse, they attempted to use decree power to put into practice economic theories in direct contravention of the spirit and purpose of the Act.

The O.P.A. was meant to hold the line on prices and costs of production, and to preserve the character and efficiency of our business system. Few people realize how close we came to destroying business.

Early in 1942 I was appointed Assistant Regional Price Executive in the San Francisco office, which was responsible for administering the Act in our nine Western states. The job did not have to be urged upon me; I had witnessed the horrors of inflation in Germany. There followed an unending fight.

The confusion was unbelievable. Contradictory directives poured out of Washington. For that matter, quite a few such bewildering orders originated in our office, too, as we tried to keep up with rapidly changing policy. Our trouble was that the economists in Washington insisted on uniform nation-wide controls, but what was appropriate for the Eastern seaboard or the South didn't necessarily apply to the West. Another difficulty stemmed from the fact that we were badly understaffed.

In the Western region, for instance, we had 548,000 square miles of territory with hundreds of widely separated population centers and 180,000 retail outlets. To administer the region there were, besides the San Francisco office, six state offices, two district offices, and an available field force, in the Price Division, of some 65 people. True, the territory boasted 600 volunteer War Price and Rationing Boards, but they were concerned largely with rationing.

And, for too long a time, the O.P.A. philosophy seemed to be to clamp a ceiling on prices and never mind production costs. As an illustration:

A ceiling of $1.95 was placed on one line of shirts. There were no controls on cotton. The price the manufacturer paid for shirting mounted. So did his labor costs and just about everything else. He shortened and cheapened his shirts, and lost money. So, in desperation, he made "sport" shirts, which were uncontrolled, to be sold at retail prices ranging up to $8.00. The consumer had to pay a high price as shirts ceased to be made at the controlled price.

This situation, in principle, was repeated many times over in different ways, almost invariably because a manufacturer or business man was caught in an impossible squeeze between his costs and what he could get for his product. Invariably the consumer took it on the chin.

Basic to the whole problem was conflict existing between the Price and Legal Divisions of the O.P.A. Legal was charged with enforcement, and a great disparity of opinion with regard to enforcement measures existed within Legal itself. By the time the conflict was partially resolved I had gone to Washington to be Assistant Deputy Administrator under Chester Bowles, who was General Manager for the agency.

In Washington there came to my attention a maneuver I can only describe as a plot to wreck our business community.

On a number of occasions I had clashed with various officials in both divisions—I will not call them Communists, but they showed the symptoms—who were resentful of business and business men. They did their best to block any reasonable solution of cost squeezes.

Finally they advanced their "solution" for the enforcement problem.

They planned to set up 3,000 war price and rationing "courts" to be manned by Leftist groups. Every business in the country was to be licensed, fifty million complaint forms printed, and three complaints could result in a business man being haled into one of their courts, to be judged by a war price "commissioner" who would have the power to deprive him of his right to operate. There was to be no appeal from the decisions of these super-judges.

The scheme was so phrased, of course, that its actual intent — to bring all industry under rigid federal control and overthrow our system of free enterprise—was concealed. It seemed so outrageous to me that I felt it could best be countered by satire. I wrote and circulated an article ridiculing aspects of the O.P.A. which had made such a radical proposal possible. Parody may not be one of my talents. Despite my efforts and those of other alarmed colleagues in the agency, the plot actually gained ground.

Finally, I discussed the situation with Senator Robert Taft of Ohio. Through his good offices the O.P.A. laws were amended to assure that no courts other than those regularly constituted could function, and to provide that courts of appeal should guarantee protection from arbitrary rulings. At the same time, additional lacks in the laws were remedied, and thenceforth O.P.A. regulations found more ready acceptance in this embattled nation.

All told, it was a miracle that price controls worked as well as they did. They depended heavily on the honesty and patriotism of the American people, and their success is mainly attributable to widespread devotion to those ideals.

My O.P.A. experience certainly proved to me that the business community should and must take a more active part in government affairs, if its interests—and those of the country as a whole—are to be protected. How easily might freedom have been lost, even while we were fighting a war for freedom!

What were the motivations of that radical group in the agency? If they were Communists (and it is well known that many such had infiltrated our government before and during the war) the answer is simple: they were obeying Party orders, and up to their usual trouble-making. Most likely some of them were Communists. But what of the others? Couldn't they realize that by robbing Americans of a fair hearing—even the business men they hated—they were attacking the very institutions that kept *them* free men? Destroy one freedom, and all other freedoms are endangered.

I've come to a few conclusions about the behavior of these voluntary saboteurs of the American way of life. In some ways it is understandable. Many Americans even share their attitudes, to some degree, and for the same reasons.

Shall we discuss briefly the condition of man in our modern era?

The last half-century has brought forth technological marvels that in my boyhood were inconceivable. They may be commonplace now, but let us mention some of them for the good of our souls.

The mass-produced automobile, super-highways, the trucking industry. Radio, television, electronics utilized in hundreds of complex and mystifying ways. The phenomenon of flight, now reckoned in terms of the speed of sound.

Late in 1959 my wife and I traveled by jet airplane from San Francisco to the Orient in eleven flying hours. It used to take us a week to get to Europe from New York by ocean liner—now New York is 8¼ hours from Paris, 7 hours from London, 14¼ hours from Buenos Aires far down in the Southern hemisphere, 4¼ hours from Caracas in Venezuela. Soon man will be rocketing into space. And, of course, there is the harnessing of the atom, at once man's dread and hope. It is a very great pity that the secrets of atomic energy were first penetrated in time of war, and that it was easiest to put it to work in a bomb. This limitless source of power, properly used, could transform the earth and liberate from drudgery all peoples inhabiting it. It is man's greatest discovery since naked, shivering ancestors of ours, eons ago, learned how to handle fire to warm themselves.

But the atomic breakthrough did come in time of war, as a result of our knowledge that German scientists were doing their utmost to develop the super-weapon, and we happened to win the race. Whether we were justified in actually employing the A-bomb will be argued until the end of time. We did, however, and we placed in the hands of mankind the power to kill on a scale of appalling magnitude.

This century of ours has aptly been called the bloodiest in history. In our era the human race has murdered more of its members, more efficiently, than at any other comparable period. This does not speak very well for human morality.

Naturally, everybody agrees that it cannot continue. We must learn to live together, all the nations of the earth, lest we exterminate ourselves. But still there is dread in the hearts of men that someone, sometime, may set off an atomic holocaust.

Mankind has succeeded, at last, in coming face to face with the ultimate in peril.

Yet this quite recent development, while it renders our situation supremely acute, does not explain the unrest, the confusion and the uncertainty among men that have led to vast dislocations and two world wars in our time. Factors contributing to unrest, confusion and uncertainty have been with us for several centuries.

For the moment, let's content ourselves with the statement that technical man has outstripped spiritual man. We have engineered a scientific and industrial complex, especially in the Western world, that is almost beyond our ability to control.

How many men understand the innards of their cars, or even the household gadgets so useful in daily living? Many more people fail to understand the intricacies of economic and political life, such as banking and the functions of corporations, or the manueverings that take place in Congress. Americans in particular have been and are bombarded continually by slanted facts through our communications media; television, radio and the press. Small wonder we are frequently confused.

Small wonder, too, that we are victims of an accelerating tendency to shift responsibility for our lives to "planners" and central authority. Only experts and bureaucrats, it is felt, can cope with the burgeoning problems of our industrial culture. To some extent, this may be true. But I would say we are going too far when, as in California, one out of every 7.3 persons in the labor force is on some public payroll—federal, state, county or municipal.

The dangers of so huge a bureaucracy are aptly illustrated by the behavior of those fellow-traveling gentry in the O.P.A. during the war. Conditioned by Socialistic ideas in the first place (as are many who gravitate to government service), they sought to put their trust in a gigantic central government that would decree every detail of American life. They sought personal advantage, also, as do all men. The point to remember is that they planned to put this scheme of theirs over on the electorate in defiance of our Constitution, without the consent of anyone other than bureaucrats, and this at untold cost to the economic health of the nation. And what were their motives?

They hated business and business men, true; but more than that, they did not believe in American democratic processes, or the heritage of freedom that has been ours for nearly 200 years. Essentially, they despised liberty.

How did they happen to be in a position to attempt such a coup?

Congress had enacted faulty laws which enabled a bureaucracy to be built up with equal haste, and inevitably unworthy public servants infiltrated. Our elected representatives had abdicated their responsibility, handing over decree powers to be wielded by the bureaucracy. They had the excuse that the nation faced the emergency of war, but more important, Congress did not want to bother with the intricacies of price control.

Our lawmakers are human, too. Many of them believe in allowing experts to handle the headaches. And something else. How do you think a Congressman or Senator feels when a mere 40% of voters turn out to cast ballots for him or his opponent? Does he represent only this many of the people?

The sad truth is that a large number of citizens in our democracy have abdicated their responsibilities and their attitude is reflected all the way up the line. A blank ballot at a voting place is not an abstention. It seems that you don't care enough about the issues at stake or you'd have used it.

It could be that this apathy in our electorate means that government of the people, by the people and for the people is about to vanish from this earth.

Before we let it vanish, it might be well to go back and trace the evolution of democracy in history and try to realize what a rare and precious possession we have in it.

II

THE DEMOCRATIC IDEA

Two opposing principles have always been at work in the thousands of attempts men have made to organize themselves into social and political systems. The principle we uphold in our American system is that government exists to serve the people. Its opposite, to which the other half of our divided world subscribes, is that the people exist to serve government.

It seems obvious which one is the more valid. We have no record of the first groups of primitive men who came together to choose the strongest or the wisest among them as leaders, but certainly they were thinking of their own welfare rather than that of the chosen.

Once a leader has tasted power, however, he develops an appetite for it. Without doubt the earliest savage chiefs quickly busied themselves figuring out ways of retaining leadership, through the support of factions within a band or tribe, or by claiming alliance with spirits and gods. This last device was apparently a favorite in keeping followers in subjection. Anthropologists tell us of many legendary priest-kings who, as social man emerged from the mists of time, reigned by means of quite highly developed religio-political systems.

Perhaps the most elaborate of these systems was that of ancient Egypt, to take a leap forward into history. The Pharaoh was divine, he inherited his divinity as well as his throne from his ancestors—by this time the natural human wish to have your children succeed to power had been sanctified by custom—and he and his family headed up a complicated hierarchy of priesthood and aristocracy. Other great systems contemporary with the Egyptian, such as the Sumerian and Assyrian civilizations, were much the same, as were still others in China and India.

It is interesting to note certain parallels between the ancient autocracies and the system obtaining in the Soviet Union today: a state "religion," Communism, which is interpreted by "priest-kings" who dwell among the desecrated churches of the Kremlin, an "aristocracy" of Party members who administer the nation and also serve as priests in spreading the religion, with a huge proletarian mass supporting the entire structure and dependent for existence on subservience to the state. Similarly, the teeming millions of China today exist in slavery.

And that was the lot of most common people in the best organized societies the ancient world could produce—slavery. Often they possessed a certain security, but if they wished to continue living they conformed to and labored for the system to which they were fettered from birth until death. Freedom had been left behind with primitive man.

About 2700 years ago, however, a new idea was born in the rocky peninsula of Greece. A sturdy people who founded a number of small city-states, the Greeks had an unusual genius for government. They believed in the basic dignity of the ordinary citizen, and considered him an intelligent being with a right to work out his own happiness. They also saw no reason why his right to happiness—his freedom— could not be guaranteed by law. Two Greek words, *demos*, the people, and *kratos*, authority, combine in the term for the system they developed, Democracy.

The Greek people exercised their authority in two ways at various times, directly as in pure democracy, and indirectly by representative government. It was in Athens that the Democratic Idea reached its fullest expression, and with it there flourished a culture that has shaped Western civilization.

But the Greeks were never able to develop a national government. Some cities, notably aristocratic and war-like Sparta, had very limited forms of democracy, or none. All the cities fought among themselves from time to time, some of them went in for empire-building, and finally Alexander the Great of Macedon embarked on his brief career of international conquest and brought an end to Greek freedom. After his death and the dissolution of his empire, the people of the peninsula actually did form a federal republic which endured a few years, but while it was democratic in theory it turned out aristocratic in fact, and it wasn't too long before the Greeks succumbed to the empire builders of Rome.

There are many reasons why Greek democracy failed to survive. For one, the Totalitarian Idea was too pervasive in the world of that time, and too many influences of Alexander's autocracy lived on in Greece, especially after his legions came home, orientalized, from as far east as India. But more basic, Greek democracy had a fatal weakness—its rights did not extend to the many slaves in peninsular cities. Even the great Greek philosophers could not seem to understand that every individual in a social organization must enjoy freedom if any are to remain free.

As a matter of fact, over 2,000 years were to pass before Abraham Lincoln enunciated the principle that *our* government could not endure half slave and half free. It applied just as aptly to the ancient Greeks.

However, the Democratic Idea did persist. It had already been transplanted from Greece to Rome—a brisk commerce existed between the two peoples — and the Roman plebian class had won political equality with the patricians in their republic. The fact that Rome possessed a compact body of citizens, equal before the law and exercising sovereign power through elected representatives, accounts largely for the development of Romans into the strongest people of their world.

The Romans were great organizers. Their genius is apparent not only in the highly efficient way they set about military conquests, but in the various forms of government they bestowed on conquered peoples. Where possible, they forced alliances on the vanquished, making dependent states of them; otherwise, seized territory was held by colonization. Eventually, most subject lands became provinces of the empire.

A particularly clever device was the granting of Roman citizenship to puppet rulers, persons of influence, or merchants. These citizens might never see Rome, nor exercise full rights, but their interests were Rome's interests and they were very useful in maintaing her power and extending her commerce. Doesn't this smack of Russia's relations with the Iron Curtain countries? Local leaders with "citizenship" — that is, membership in the Communist Party — thrust into power by force, so as to control satellite peoples for the benefit of Moscow? Indeed, there is little new under the sun.

The Roman republican government did not survive the forging of the empire. Long before the sway of Rome reached around the Mediterranean Sea and north into Europe, only the forms of republicanism remained. The empire was ruled by an aristocracy, the vast majority of its peoples either submerged economically or actually enslaved. The Totalitarian Idea once more triumphed completely when Rome became an imperial monarchy with supreme authority vested in a succession of Caesars. Freedom had vanished, and it was not to reappear in the world for a very long time.

Only Christianity kept the idea of individual liberty alive. Christ's promise of salvation to all the humble of the earth, energetically spread by evangelists of the early church, enabled oppressed peoples to achieve spiritual freedom even though personal and political freedom were denied them.

And as the worldly empire of Rome decayed, its dissolution brought about as much by its own corruptness as by the turbulent and predatory peoples assaulting its borders, the spiritual empire of Christ grew. By the year 500 most former Roman lands were Christianized. Even invaders assumed the Cross. Governments were autocratic and the church, inevitably involved in political tides, itself became somewhat corrupt, but it served its purpose.

Through all His teachings there shone the concept of the worth and dignity of the individual. As long as men held to this truth, its corollary—that somewhere, sometime, all men could achieve political freedom—would remain a cherished dream never entirely suppressed.

The so-called Dark Ages that next fell over Europe were not as black as we imagine. Social strata were rigidly frozen, overall rule was exercised by an aristocracy, commerce was conducted by a class, and the structure was fed by a serfdom, it is true. But nearly everyone enjoyed some economic security, despite political maneuverings and wars, and men's souls were strengthened by a devout belief in God. What evils might assail them in this life would be recompensed in a glorious Hereafter, under conditions prescribed by the church.

Few significant advances were made by medieval man—indeed, he seems to have "slept" for about 600 years insofar as contributions to European culture were concerned. But when he awakened in the Renaissance it was to begin a revolution which has continued ever since.

First he reached back into the past, enthusiastically rediscovering the achievements of Greece and Rome. Then, men of the Renaissance, breaking with tradition, strove for new horizons in art, in science, in philosophy, in politics, and in commerce. A fresh concept in finance, Capitalism, by which money itself became a commodity for the getting of more money, wrought changes in commerce particularly. And, at the end of the fifteenth century, a whole new world was opened to exploitation by capitalism as the Americas were discovered.

The idea of political freedom next fermented in Europe, sparked by the rebellion of Martin Luther and John Calvin against the traditional church. It had had an earlier genesis; as far back as 1215 the barons of England had forced the Magna Carta from a reluctant King John, laying the basis for English constitutional liberty. But the rights thus won did not reach down through the ranks of society to do very much for the common man. Among commoners, the revolutionary spirit first took a religious turn—the word Protestant has a twofold meaning. While not ceasing to be devout, common people were protesting restraints political as well as religious in seizing upon new doctrines which offered equality within a congregation.

Totalitarian forces of repression were quick to recognize the political significances in religious revolt—Protestants were persecuted. Then a solution: let the rebels populate the new world, along with adventurers, other restless malcontents, and minor criminals. Get rid of the whole troublesome pack.

The European colonial powers, England and France particularly, in this way purged themselves of some of their best blood—forward-looking people who sought freedom—freedom of religion and of speech, freedom from want, and from fear. It is interesting to note that the way to freedom was opened more often than not by private companies made up of weathly men with surplus funds to invest, i.e., capitalists. It took capital to found colonies, and to nurture them so they could grow and return profits in trade to the mother countries.

These companies, their mission completed, had been dissolved by the time our American Revolution began brewing. But the concept that colonies existed for the benefit of the homeland—in our case, England — remained. The colonists rejected this notion. They considered themselves Englishmen, with the rights of Englishmen. And more, their leaders were deeply imbued with the Democratic Idea .

This had been restated, a few decades before 1775, by the French philosopher Rousseau in his writings about Natural Man. It was the old Greek idea, amplified. It inspired Tom Paine, the tempestuous pamphleteer who played such a large part in precipitating our ideological break with Great Britain.

Actually, the English yoke was very light on these colonies, and many Americans felt that Paine far exceeded the bounds of *Common Sense*, as he called his first incendiary paper, in his denunciations of the Crown. But Paine later uttered a profound truth when he said: "The independence of America, considered merely as a separation from England, would have been a matter of but little importance, had it not been accompanied by a revolution in the principles and practices of government. She made a stand, not for herself only, but for the world."

Indeed, the Declaration of Independence went beyond the plain needs of the moment when Thomas Jefferson penned the following words:

"We hold these truths to be self-evident, that all men are created equal, that they are endowed by their Creator with certain inalienable rights, that among these are life, liberty and the pursuit of happiness. That to secure these rights, governments are instituted among men, deriving their just powers from the consent of the governed. That whenever any form of government becomes destructive of these ends, it is the right of the people to alter or abolish it, and to institute new government, laying its foundations on such principles and organizing its powers in such form, as to them shall seem most likely to effect their safety and happiness."

Jefferson and others of our founding fathers, however, had felt the need to lay hold on universal human principles. As a result, the American message rang out across oceans to lands far from our shores. One is tempted to compare it with Christ's message of universal spiritual freedom.

Of course, the mere sending of a message doesn't guarantee its acceptance. Our forebears had to fight for six hard and disheartening years against the British government (not the British people, most of whom hated the war) to make the message stick even for themselves. And then they had to write the Constitution and make *that* stick with all the 13 colonies, despite vigorous movements for a monarchy, and for restriction of voting rights to people of property.

It was, in fact, years before everybody in this country could vote. Some of our states operated on a slave-based economy until the Civil War was fought. But we started working things out in the cause of freedom for all a long time ago, and while there is still ground to be gained in places, notably the fields of social and economic discrimination, we do have the governmental machinery to continue working.

Let's sum up what we have in practical terms:

A freely elected government responsible to all the people, with the powers of its branches—executive, legislative and judicial.

A system of individual rights established by law, including freedom of speech, freedom of religion, freedom of the press, and protection against arbitrary arrest and imprisonment without due process of law.

An economic system whereby an individual can choose his work and stay with it as he pleases, change it, or go in for free enterprise if he feels so inclined.

In exercising these rights, we naturally have an obligation not to intrude on the rights of others; and further, we have the opportunity as well as a responsibility to cooperate freely as citizens, as most of us always have and still do.

A quote from a French traveler, Alexis de Tocqueville, describes us quite well. In the 1830's, he wrote:

"These Americans are the most peculiar people in the world. You'll not believe it when I tell you how they behave. In a local community

in their country a citizen may conceive of some need which is not
being met. What does he do? He goes across the street and discusses
it with his neighbor. Then what happens? A committee comes into
existence and then the committee begins functioning on behalf of that
need, and you won't believe this but it's true. All of this is done
without reference to any bureaucrat. All of this is done by the
private citizens on their own initiative.

"Americans of all ages, all conditions, and all dispositions consis-
tently form associations . . . to give entertainments, to found semi-
naries, to build inns, to construct churches, to diffuse books, to send
missionaries to the Antipodes . . .

"The health of a democratic society may be measured by the quality
of functions performed by private citizens."

Certainly not the least of American freedoms is that by which we
may improve ourselves and remedy social lacks.

We may take these freedoms for granted, but do you realize that
they have been achieved, in America and the Western world, only in
the last two centuries in a recorded history of more than 5,000 years?
Think *that* over.

The beauty of democratic systems is that they provide an opportunity for humanity to grow. Thomas Jefferson once remarked that
a nation needs a revolution about every twenty-five years or so, and
he and the other framers of our Constitution saw to it that we could
have our revolutions by peaceful means—by elections, politically.
He could hardly have foreseen the economic and social revolutions we
have undergone since his time, but these were assured a peaceful outcome by our free political system.

Could the expansion, settlement and development of our country to
the Pacific Coast have been achieved by other than free men? I
doubt it. Of course, we were protected by geographic isolation from
the rest of the world during our most spectacular period of growth.
But it was the emigrating manpower of Europe, men seeking a free
country, that in the 1800's filled the Mississippi Valley and the West,
and built these regions up in a few generations.

How extremely fortunate we have been in the wealth of human
material we have received in this country! But then, the people have
always known what they wanted, especially the strong, the enterpris-
ing, the young. Freedom, and opportunity. Opportunity afforded only
by a young, captalist land.

By tens of thousands, farmers plowed the soil, miners delved in the earth, woodsmen worked the forest. Small businesses proliferated, serving the needs of thousands of embryonic communities. A man could start on the proverbial shoestring. He might have to work hard, but he could grow with the place where he put down his roots, as he can still.

In the days of our expansion, capitalism did practice its excesses, especially in the fields of railroading, mining, oil production, steel-making, and finance. But capital was used in a predatory fashion all over the world then, and quite soon the American people, led by Theodore Roosevelt, curbed the power of big corporations through the anti-trust laws. The Democratic Idea was at work, and a principle embodied in the Declaration of Independence was extended: ". . . whenever any form of government (political or economic) becomes destructive of these ends (life, liberty and the pursuit of happiness), it is the right of the people to alter or abolish it . . ."

Business is a form of government in our economic lives, and it requires regulation. The old Romans, who bequeathed us many of our legal concepts—especially the notion of incorporation—recognized this in their laws regarding property and inheritance. In our system we have gone much further. A modern corporation, made up of men but designed to endure even though the men may come and go, is possessed of the rights of an individual, and also of an individual's responsibilities insofar as its activities affect the rights and well-being of others. But a corporation wields much more power than any individual, these days. Who will deny that General Motors, to take an instance, has the power to affect the lives of every one of us? It is this fact that led an officer of that company to remark that what was good for General Motors was good for the country.

His observation brought a hoot of derision from many people, because an outdated idea of business as predatory persists in America. Actually, in many ways the man was right. Imagine how our economy would limp along *without* G.M. What would the country have done in World War II without the manifold services of that industrial colossus?

The truth is that America's corporations, almost without exception, are fully aware of their social responsibilities—and if at any time they are not, the U.S. Department of Justice is vigilant in guarding against any overstepping of bounds.

A very important question is now appropriate: Who owns DuPont and General Motors? The answer: Thousands upon thousands of ordinary American citizens who have invested in the stocks of those corporations. As a matter of fact, nearly twelve and one-half million individuals in this country now own shares in public corporations! That's one out of every eight American adults. Is this Capitalism in the classic sense? It is rather a People's Capitalism.

Many corporations encourage ownership by employees, for example, Sears, Roebuck & Co. About 26% of Sears' stock (nearly twenty million shares) have been acquired over the years by Sears people through a savings and profit-sharing program. No employee member may contribute more than $500 a year, so as to keep the high-salaried from taking over. In 1958 a truck driver who retired after forty-four working years received $289,000. His contribution to the Sears fund totaled $5,928. Such can be the financial rewards of free enterprise in our economy.

Ownership of industry by the people isn't confined to holding stock directly, by any means. There are some seventy million Americans who have insurance policies, and their premiums must be invested, partly in industry. Millions more have a stake in pension plans, group insurance plans, union funds, etc., and this money is kept busy. The International Ladies' Garment Workers Union has for years made a practice of lending capital to manufacturers in that line—and the members of the union have enjoyed not only their share of profits but more and steadier employment.

Indeed, the American Capitalist is the man on the street, or the retired worker, or his widow.

Consider also the many measures for personal security that have grown up in our time: workmen's compensation, unemployment insurance, social security and old age benefits, accident and health insurance, veterans' benefits and insured education plans, etc.

If Karl Marx were to return to earth and see what a democracy with reasonably free enterprise has achieved in curing the social ills he cried out against, he would be confounded. He might even admit he was wrong.

Our system is not perfect. It has its inequities and injustices, but it is a system of opportunities to improve ourselves.

The outlook for the future poses more problems as our industrial culture becomes more complicated. Efficiency demands big units of production, big distribution, big government, and great power concentrated in the hands of a few hundred corporations, in the agencies of central political control. We must be efficient if we are to maintain our place in the world. Will we sacrifice our freedoms to bigness in order to be efficient?

Such a choice should never become necessary. Whatever faults our system possesses, it does assure the most important freedom of all—freedom to grow in directions desired by the American people.

What is the destiny of man if not to change, to adapt and to find fuller expression of himself, generation by generation? Albert Schweitzer has voiced the idea that we have been given life in order to struggle closer and closer to God's perfection. Not all men may wish to accept this, but surely no man wants to relinquish his right to move closer to his own idea of perfection. We have that right under our system, both as individuals and as a people.

International Communism, on the other hand, is essentially restrictive in its ideology. It seeks to freeze mankind at the present stage of development and to arrest all progress except along material lines dictated by the Party. This is a strange and bewildering thing when the future of men could be so bright with promise.

Shall we try to discover the reasons for this malignant attitude and trace something of its development?

III

THE TOTALITARIAN IDEA

Along with the ferment for political freedom that was a-yeasting as Europe emerged into the modern era in the 17th and 18th centuries, another movement began to gain followers—Socialism. This was perhaps an inevitable offshoot of Rousseau's philosophy, which possessed some extremely radical aspects; but more, the rapacities of classic Capitalism fostered resentment in behalf of the exploited laboring class.

Capitalists held that money made industry possible, and therefore capital should reap the great reward. Labor was merely a commodity in the process of production, to be bought and employed more or less like raw material, iron or cotton. The Industrial Revolution helped to reveal to most thinking individuals that this conception was harsh and inhuman.

James Watt's great improvements on the steam engine, in the late 1700's, ushered in the so-called machine age. Men had built and used machines for centuries before this; but now, with steam affording a cheap and efficient source of power, all sorts of new machines could be used in manufacturing, multiplying production many times, and employment as well.

This was revolution, indeed, adding to the complexities of an age of poiltical revolution. We mustn't forget that while Watt was busily erecting his early steam engines, our revolution was being fought; that while steam was being used in the grinding of grain and the weaving of cloth on the power loom, the French Revolution burst on a startled world.

The revolution of the French was a bourgeois movement, actually, engineered by the educated and propertied class for its own benefit, though it used many laborers as fighters. And French monarchic autocracy was overthrown only temporarily; reaction set in with the dictatorship of Napoleon, a bourgeois who assumed the trappings of aristocracy and empire.

But the Totalitarian Idea, as it then obtained in Europe, was having serious trouble. The mass armies Napoleon needed in his career of conquest were composed of common men, and even he enacted laws that guaranteed civil liberties of sorts for all the French people. These were retained in the monarchies that followed his fall. Meanwhile, other European governments were rapidly being liberalized.

As a natural outgrowth of political libertarianism, the economic condition of the laboring classes was bound to receive attention. The socialists of Europe were right in the swing of things, and while they encountered resistance from government and capitalists, they were at least free to express their theories—as they did, openly and vigorously.

Socialistic ideas were far from new. There is a strong element of socialism, even communism, in basic Christianity. And, for centuries, men had been dreaming of ideal forms of society which would eliminate the evils of the social orders in which they happened to find themselves.

As far back as 400 B.C. the old Greek philosopher Plato spoke of a "perfect" small state in which, though most of the work would be done by slaves, a select few would lead virtuous, contemplative lives. St. Augustine advocated the abolition of private property in his *City of God*. Sir Thomas More is probably the best known of idealistic planners; his *Utopia*, published in 1416, has given a name to all similar works that have followed, and there have been many Utopians.

Whether seriously proposed or not, these schemes are a lot of fun to read. And it is useful to note that almost every one of them possesses an outstanding feature: the members of a supposedly ideal society must conform to rigid standards of conduct of one sort or another, highly moral or—by our standards—frankly immoral, as the case may be. No deviation whatever is tolerated.

Isn't it strange that the majority of those who would reform the human race insist that it can be accomplished by the surrender of individual liberty, by the imposition of their ideas on other men?

This is not to imply that all Socialists are out-and-out totalitarians or that their efforts toward security for humanity are undesirable. However, there is an element of the Totalitarian Idea in nearly every Socialist proposal, ironically, whether it be sweeping or small. We might remember that Mussolini and Hitler began as Socialists of differing stripe.

The most pervasive Socialist idea of our time, Marxist Communism, was totalitarian from its concept. It came into being along with dozens of other notions in the first half of the nineteenth century and briefly dominated them. Communism, however, was strong medicine. Like anarchism and nihilism, it advocated utter destruction of existing systems, and milder Socialists soon drew away from it. Marxism, in fact, is hardly Socialistic at all, considering it practically. It is merely revolutionary, the weird product of a neurotic, anti-social mind, though an extremely brilliant mind.

Karl Marx, born in 1818, grew up in a disunited politics-plagued Germany. He was subjected to many disturbing influences and undoubtedly suffered psychologically. Heinrich Marx, his father, had much to do with the development of Karl's mentality, but he could exercise little to restrain his son. At the University of Berlin, then a hotbed for all kinds of radicalism, young Marx became a militant atheist and a political rebel. These bents were hardly appropriate for the official career he had planned so he gave up law and turned to philosophy, eventually receiving a doctor's degree from the University of Jena. A series of rebuffs embittered him. He lost a promised lectureship at the University of Bonn. He became editor of a newspaper in Cologne and his radical articles brought about its suppression. He escaped to Paris, took part in another ill-fated journalistic venture, and, falling under the influence of anarchists there, developed into a revolutionary.

During this period, Marx formed the only two lasting relationships of his life. He married the patient girl who had already waited seven years for him and who willingly shared an existence of exile, poverty and protest. Early in 1844 he made friends with Friedrich Engels, the collaborator who supported him financially off and on until his death.

Engels, two years younger than the gloomy Marx, had been born to wealth and was already a partner in the Manchester, England, branch of his family's cotton manufacturing firm. However, he was as radical as Marx and equally responsible for their most celebrated work, the *Communist Manifesto*, a work written as a sort of political platform for the Communist League, a society in which Marx and Engels were the leading spirits and propagandists. It is curious how two such well-educated men could have given birth to so much astoundingly faulty theory.

But before appraising basic Communist doctrine, let's examine the situation in Europe in 1848. It has a lot to do with what went into the *Manifesto*.

The continent was seething with rebellion. A series of little revolutions in 1830—in France, Belgium (this the lone success, in that the Belgians won their independence from the Dutch), Italy, Germany and Poland—had been quelled, largely. But all through the succeeding years, secret political societies flourished, led by all manner of socialist and anarchist plotters. By the late 1840's, another revolution was felt due in France; the French revolt of 1830 had set off the others.

The condition of labor in industry was frankly terrible. Children worked long hours in coal mines, foundries and factories. Women and girls made bricks. Homes where lace and cloth were made were sweatshops. Laborers' dwellings were overcrowded, unsanitary; whole families lived in one room. Ignorance, vice, crime and disease prevailed among the poor, and the death rate climbed higher every year.

These conditions were not necessarily universal. There were many fairly humane employers, and some who actually strove to improve their workers' lot, according to their lights. But by and large, things were anything but good.

Marx and Engels conceived of European society as one class opposed against another—the exploiters and the exploited. The bourgeoisie against the proletariat. Property owners versus the dispossessed. Actually, the facts did not justify so sweeping a generalization even then. While industry had become concentrated, employing a large class of workers exploited in varying degrees, there were still many small employers, people who worked at their own enterprises alongside their employees. These Marx and Engels brushed off. Independent small farmers they likewise ignored. All these were both exploiters and the exploited, the agents of capitalism and its victims. The middle class would quickly vanish, in any event, absorbed in the proletariat.

The most important fact about Marx and Engels is that they didn't want to believe in anything but class warfare. They didn't want to look ahead or put any faith in the processes of social evolution, in the ability of men—however slowly—to eradicate injustices and correct evils.

They wanted to flip the world over right then, in 1848. They wanted to be the leaders of this proletariat they envisioned as rising bloodily to seize power—which would be handed over to them. They were bitterly disappointed.

The revolutions of 1848, begun in France and continued in other countries, did not succeed nor even arouse the proletariat, that submerged lower class they never really troubled to define. Marx and Engels did their best to direct the upheavels from Brussels, from Paris, from Cologne. The next year, they fled to London, where Marx was finally settled in the ill-lighted rooms where he tried all his

life to fortify the false principles of the *Manifesto* with his *Capital,*
three volumes of turgid prose high-lighted by slashing hate.

No question about it: this man was brilliant. But a fervent
admirer put his finger squarely on Marx's severest lacks when he
wrote of him: "If his heart were as big as his brain and his love as
great as his hate I would go through fire for him, despite the fact
that he indicated his low opinion of me. . . . He is the first and
only one amongst us to whom I would ascribe the quality of leadership, the capacity to master a big situation without losing himself
in insignificant details."

Still another revolutionary colleague described him as 'perfidious
and malicious.' If Marx were the best they could offer in the way
of a leader, no wonder their movement almost died with him in 1883.

As for his abhorrence of 'details,' let us see how this quality led
him into gross errors of reasoning.

Marx borrowed his method of thought, dialectics, from Hegel, another mixed-up philosopher. This seems to be a process of argument
by which a truth is found, an anti-truth discovered denying it, and
a double-negatived truth frightened out of cover by synthesis between
the truth and anti-truth.

Dialectics is a most convenient tool for a wishful thinker—you
can 'prove' nearly anything with it, without much regard for facts.
That's probably why it appealed to Marx.

Conceiving that the proletariat of Europe was ripe for the seizure
of power from bourgeois ascendancy, because he wished that to
happen, he sought to interpret all history from the standpoint of
'dialectical materialism': that is, he claimed that all historical change
had come about through economic class warfare, which simply isn't
true. Many other forces have affected the course of history—climate,
growth and decline of populations, plagues, international trade, and
just plain conquest—not to mention the manipulations of leaders.

Marx foretold the 'dictatorship of the proletariat,' in itself a fan-
tastic phrase. It is meant to convey a picture of triumphant dominance to the downtrodden, but its very words are mutually exclusive.
Dictatorship is exercised by one man or a group of men; how can the
masses dictate? 'Every man a king' is just about as silly a concept.
If all are kings, who are the subjects?

Of course, Marx meant that dictatorship would be the function of
proletarian leaders—he said as much—who would desert the ranks of
the bourgeois class to confer the inestimable benefits of their services

on the workers. And, by this, Marx meant Marx, and others like him.

In 1867, still hoping, he wrote to Engels: "Things are moving. And in the next revolution, which is perhaps nearer than it appears, *we will have this powerful engine in our hands.*" But neither then, nor later, did it happen for Marx.

And what was to have been the outcome of the dictatorship of the proletariat?

The sway of the workers, implemented by their leaders, would be only temporary, Marx prophesied. Then, when everybody had learned to appreciate the blessings of socialism, when there was no more private property of any description and all greed and self-seeking had been extirpated from the hearts of men, there would come into being a 'classless' society and the state would 'wither away.' There would be no need for government, since conditions for the existence of classes and of class antagonisms would have vanished. And the credo of society would be: "From each according to his abilities, to each according to his needs."

Marxists indignantly deny that there is anything in the least utopian about Marxism—but this vision, I fear, is a utopian gem of the clearest water. Not that I wouldn't like to see such a society, composed of perfect men.

However, Marx didn't believe in this fatuous cloud-cuckoo-land, either. Elsewhere he speaks quite vehemently of 'permanent revolution'—an idea which came to mean world revolution under Lenin—and he apparently saw nothing beyond that. This man, with his hates, certainly couldn't credit that all men might become perfect within the foreseeable future.

Of his economic preachments regarding the 'labor theory of value' and 'surplus value' we need to say little. In many, many thousands of words he attempted to prove that only the worker's contribution to production possessed value, and that capital created no value at all. The fact that capital and labor together were in his own lifetime creating the greatest prosperity the world had yet seen, meant nothing to him.

As for his prophecy that the middle class would disappear—it grew in strength while he watched and has gone on gaining ever since.

He promised that, with concentration of industry, capital would be gathered into the hands of fewer and fewer men—and capital ownership has spread through entire nations.

He insisted that, without a revolution, the proletariat would sink more and more deeply into exploited misery—and the condition of labor has improved until it often receives by far the greatest share in the rewards of production.

He selected England as the country most likely to spawn a purely proletarian revolution—and the people of England finally repudiated socialism overwhelmingly.

How could Marx have been so wrong? More to the point, how can Communists today hold Marxian doctrine to be absolute gospel? Part of the answer is that dialectical materialism can be used to prove anything. Remember? And Marx has been explained to the faithful since his day with so much double-thinking gobbledygook that his errors have been obscured. Communist doctrine is what its high priests dictate, since Lenin took hold of it.

But what is the appeal of Communism? Why does this repressive ideology attract so many ardent devotees?

Its basic theory, to begin with, is ostensibly socialistic—and for youth especially the ideal of a utopian society in which all have absolute economic equality still wields its magic. Idealists in general seem to reject fact in favor of theory, anyway.

Many turn their backs on the false prophets of Communism as they grow older and disillusionment sets in. Witness the number of Party members in this country who have recanted in middle age. But for others, mainly the neurotic, the demand of Leninist Communism for discipline and selfless dedication to the cause has its own peculiar appeal.

These people, like Marx, emotionally lopsided, nourish within themselves a hatred of humanity, the result of psychological injuries which have warped them. The very violence of revolutionary preachment is food for their sick souls. They accept the tortuous reversals of the Party line because they prefer not to think for themselves; much of the security the revolutionary fellowship affords stems from the fact that individual thinking is forbidden. Moreover, the faithful are promised a share in Party power when the great day dawns.

Yes, the appeal of Communism to its die-hards is essentially totalitarian. What these people seek is power, power for revenge, power they can attain in no other way than by forcibly placing themselves above their fellow men.

Certainly this was the motivation of Nicolai Lenin, when he sought a tool he could use to elevate himself to leadership of Russia's faceless millions.

IV

HOW COMMUNISM SEIZED RUSSIA

Interestingly enough, Marx and Engels considered Russia the least promising of European nations for their proletarian revolt. Communist theory as evolved by them held that such an uprising must come first in a highly developed industrial society, like England's or ours. Indeed, they profoundly distrusted Russia, correctly construing Tsarist policy as having but one aim—world domination.

Communist Russia today is not so very different from Tsarist Russia of the past few centuries, as a matter of fact. Some of the reasons are to be found in the country's history.

The Russians were late in acquiring the European culture that grew out of the Renaissance. During the Dark Ages they were a semi-savage people paying tribute to the Mongols and Tartars of Asia. Not until the fifteenth century did the Dukes of Moscow throw off the oriental yoke—only to continue the practice of Oriental absolutism in government. They bequeathed their belief in the Totalitarian Idea to the Tsars.

The next two centuries saw the Muscovites still forging a feudalistic empire. Russia was the only European nation able to expand by conquering barbarian lands. And, in this process, she enslaved her own peasant population as serfs, rewarding her military commanders with vast estates, together with the labor to work them. By the 1700's, the conditions of the people were truly pitiful. Peter the Great, forward-looking only in that he turned part of his enormous energy to the importing of Western technology, gave Russia the forms of a modern state but changed nothing of its actual despotism.

But the libertarian movement in Europe did have echoes in Russia. In the nineteenth century, Tsar Alexander II in particular instituted some reforms, granting Russia's serfs personal freedom by his edict of 1861. By 1915 about half of Russia's peasants owned their farms—a situation that proved highly objectionable to the Communists a few years later.

Communism is relatively recent in Russia. True, Tsarist autocracy bred many revolutionists, but Marx doesn't seem to have been too popular with them. There were dozens, if not hundreds of other rebel cults throughout the country at the dawn of the twentieth century. Their doctrines ranged all the way from nihilism and anarchism through myriad socialist notions to proposals for mere constitutional monarchy. Hopes for this last had been dashed when, in 1881, Alexander II was assassinated by a Nihilist just as he had authorized the setting up of a national legislature, the Duma.

Exactly when Nicolai Lenin seized on Marxian doctrine is hard to say. But he became a professional revolutionist at an early age, perhaps motivated by hatred that had its birth when an older brother was hanged. In 1895 Lenin himself was exiled to Siberia for anti-government activities. Returning to Russia in 1900, he soon departed to do his plotting against the Tsar from safer regions in Europe.

Many other Communists were in exile. Promptly Lenin assumed leadership of the newly formed Bolshevik wing of the Party, and became its principal theorist. The Bolsheviks believed that the dictatorship of the proletariat could become a reality in Russia without going through the phases of developing a high order of industrial society. More orthodox Marxians, the Mensheviks, advocated a procedure that would permit a transitory capitalism to exist before beginning the extermination of the bourgeois class.

Possibly more basic to Party conflict was the insistence of Lenin and his cronies that power should be concentrated in the hands of hard-core professionals like themselves, and that the rigid discipline of an army should reach down through the lowest ranks. Lenin wrote reams on Party organization, strategy and tactics, trying to turn it into his own instrument.

Both Bolsheviks and Mensheviks expected great things of the 1905 revolution. Lenin did his best to mastermind this more or less spontaneous uprising of Navy, workers and peasants from a headquarters in Finland, then part of Russia. But Nicholas II managed to retain his throne and preserve power for the monarchists by promising reforms, including a written constitution and a Duma. The bloody year ended with nearly three million freedom fighters laying down their arms. A most disgruntled Lenin was exiled again in 1907 ,to spend the better part of the next ten years in Switzerland.

Probably there never would have been a Red Revolution except for the tragedy of World War I. Though Lenin and the Bolsheviks frenziedly plotted and agitated for proletarian revolt, and to some extent infiltrated the Navy, Army and Russian trade unions, the vast majority of their countrymen looked on the Tsar as a species of father—and Nicholas II actually did succeed in improving the national political climate.

But Germany declared war in 1914, and the debacle that gave Russia to the Communist totalitarians had begun.

By the winter of 1916-17, the Russian armies had practically collapsed. Leaders in the Duma, none of them Bolsheviks, few of them even Mensheviks, forced the Tsar's abdication and set up a moderate provisional government they hoped would work out something like England's. Alexander Kerensky, the patriot head of the Social Revolutionary Party, took over in May, 1917, and vigorously resumed the war against Germany.

Prior to this libertarian revolution, hundreds of bitter soldiers and sailors had turned Bolshevik and deserted. The German generals, in particular Ludendorff, were well aware of the disruptive Bolshevik potential. Lenin had been refused Allied permission to travel to Russia when the revolution broke out. So Ludendorff had him smuggled out of Switzerland and through Germany in a sealed train, on Lenin's promise of collaboration. Not that Ludendorff had any Bolshevik leanings—he just wanted Russia out of the war.

Lenin delivered in time—his own time. At first the Bolsheviks were not strong enough to unhorse Kerensky—there were fewer than 30,000 of them in a nation of 141 million people. They were highly organized, however. Aided by that military genius, Leon Trotsky (who had hurried home from America), and hatchet man Josef Stalin (returned from a sentence in Siberia as a bank robber), Lenin recruited Bolshevik ranks to perhaps 80,000, and meanwhile laid the groundwork for a coup d'etat, all in the greatest secrecy.

The Red reactionary counter-revolution—and that is what is was, despite Communist denials — struck on the evening of November 7, 1918, or October 25th by the old Russian calendar. Railway, telegraph and telephone systems began to be seized as rapidly as possible. Before dawn, Red troops occupied government buildings and key points throughout Petrograd. All the ministers were captured except Kerensky, who escaped.

The reason for the timing of the October Revolution was that the All-Russian Congress of Soviets, the councils of workers that had sprung up all over the country, was scheduled to meet in Petrograd on the 25th. That day, Lenin told the delegates he had control of the city. The next day, he forced recognition of his Council of People's Commissars as the government of Russia. This was the "dictatorship of the proletariat"—rammed down the throats of the workers' leaders.

The Bolsheviks did not quite dare to halt the general elections already planned by the provisional government. They were roundly defeated, winning only 175 out of 707 seats in the Constituent Assembly. When its members met in January, 1918, Lenin broke up the first session with hoodlums; and as the representatives of the people gathered for the second on the following day, Red troops denied them entrance to the meeting hall. There was nothing to do but go home. Russia hasn't seen a free election since.

The present Russian leaders would like us to forget these events. After all, they happened some forty years ago.

And indeed we might, if there were any real indication that the basic aims of Bolshevik Communism have been changed. So far, we have received no satisfactory proof even of intent to change. The situation has been extended on a global scale, that's all, with changes in strategy.

Thus it will be useful to examine developments since the October Revolution.

The old Bolsheviks had no easy time of it. Abroad, Lenin's grandiose dream of a world revolution, to be touched off by his Russian coup, failed of achievement everywhere. Moreover, his surrender to the Germans caused an enraged reaction among Russia's war-time allies, and Trotsky's Red Army soon had to fend off foreign attacks. At the same time a civil war of five years' duration beset the totalitarians.

However, the war-weary Allies had no great will to win, and the army and the secret police gradually quelled internal opposition. Some twenty million Russians were killed or starved to death during the Red Terror and the period of chaos that ensued after it. The Bolsheviks were firmly in the saddle by 1922. Now the leaders turned to fighting among themselves.

There had been opposition to Lenin's policies, even from top Bolsheviks. Some of these had resigned and fled, others were still around—and dangerous principally for Stalin, who had risen to become General Secretary of the Party and Lenin's chief lieutenant in the Politburo, the inner circle of dictators. The trial of twenty-two prominent Social Revolutionaries who had collaborated with the Bolsheviks signaled the beginning of terror in the higher echelons.

Belatedly Lenin tried to stop Stalin, recognizing that this paladin of pure power who had been so useful to him was a threat to the principles of revolution as he had conceived them. But Lenin was a sick man, certain to die. His protests were of no avail, he could not engineer Stalin's removal as General Secretary, nor could he even prevent Stalin's badgering of his wife. The victim of gang rule he himself had established, Lenin died of a final stroke in January, 1924.

It took Stalin more than two years to demote Trotsky, and longer to have him exiled. Then, patiently scheming and maneuvering, he proceeded against other old comrades, great and small. The famous Party purges of the 1930's became a stench in the nostrils of the world.

Khrushchev has given us the figures in his 1956 denunciation of Stalin: 98 out of 139 members of the Central Committee arrested and shot, 1,108 of 1,966 members of the 17th Party Congress seized to suffer a variety of fates. Stalin exiled, murdered or drove to suicide all of his pals in the original Politburo. In purges of the military services it is estimated that 30,000 officers died.

But Stalin's crimes against the Russian people are of most interest to us.

In his time trade unions, already deprived of the right to strike, became instruments of government for the degradation of labor. Collective bargaining forbidden, men were harnessed to their machines, work norms were enforced, and infractions of rules could be punished by loss of food cards, eviction of a sinner and his family from their home, and sentencing to a "corrective labor camp."

The establishment of the slave labor camp system is an incredible thing. There were more than 800 of them finally, and nobody knows how many unfortunates they held. Estimates run between fifteen and thirty million prisoners, many of them farmers who objected to giving up their land.

Successive "plans" for agriculture enforced collectivization of farms, reducing the peasants to much the same state of serfdom as under the old Tsars. Uncooperative Ukrainians to the number of five million were deported or deliberately let starve to death. Or were hanged.

Soviet industry did make great strides forward under Stalin, the God-Emperor who insisted on deifying himself—it is largely due to Stalin that Russia had become the second most powerful nation in the world. Ironically, he fulfilled Marx's more important prophecies about our democratic system of enterprise in forging the "state capitalism" which is actually the system on which the U.S.S.R. operates.

Marx said that more and more capitalistic power would be concentrated in the hands of fewer and fewer men — this has happened in Russia. He said that the proletariat would sink more and more deeply into exploited misery. That class warfare would result from conflict between the exploited and the repressive bourgeoisie.

Stalin definitely created a bourgeois class in Russia, replacing that liquidated by the old Bolsheviks—the "new class" that manages everything from upper levels of government down to the lower orders of foremanship in the factories and collective farms.

However, that any uprising of the proletariat will come of "class warfare" in this situation is highly doubtful. The dictatorship is still too firmly in the saddle and the "subversion" practiced by the dictators and their new class too widespread among its victims, the entire Soviet people. In fact, if there had been any possibility of a counter-revolution, it would have come during World War II, which Stalin managed to convert into a personal triumph.

V

WORLD WAR II — A RUSSIAN VICTORY

My wife was in Berlin on the fateful Saturday in March 1933, when Hitler made himself dictator of Germany. On Sunday, she witnessed the terror that Nazi Storm Troopers visited on the Jews; shops and synagogues demolished, defenseless men and women shot and beaten, and others hauled away to prison and torture. It seemed to her as if humanity had suddenly gone mad.

Camille Perrin, a Parisian associate of our company and a graduate of St. Cyr (his nation's West Point) was told by the French Ambassador to get out of Germany—war was coming. That Hitler could be permitted to arm the Germans was unthinkable. Yet an idiotic world stood aside while he did exactly that for the next six years.

Much reproach has been heaped on the head of a certain umbrella-bearing prime minister for negotiating the Munich pact with Hitler. But that was in 1938, and he was merely voicing the belief of his world when he said there would be "peace in our time." However, this appeasement of the Fuehrer did make war inevitable, for it convinced Stalin that the Germans could whip the spineless Western democracies.

A shrewd and crafty man, Stalin—not one to be caught on the losing side. He signed his non-aggression pact with Hitler on August 23, 1939, and a week later gobbled up his share of territory when the Germans tested their blitzkrieg tactics against Poland. World War II was on, and Stalin had started it just as much as Hitler.

For the next two years, almost, Russian grain and oil flowed into Germany while Hitler overran most of Western Europe. Of course, Stalin made time on his own during the Nazi rampage. He invaded spunky Finland and, after officially making friends with Estonia, Latvia and Lithuania so as to open those little countries to Soviet troops, he annexed them. The career of Russia as a modern colonial power had begun.

Perhaps Stalin figured that if he let the Axis chew up the rest of the world for him, global revolution would be that much closer. He got the nastiest surprise of his life when Hitler, misjudging the Red Army by the poor showing it had made against the heroic Finns, invaded Russia.

He shouldn't have been surprised. Hitler had long made it plain in speech and writing that he wanted the Russian heartland, and that he considered the U.S.S.R. a menace to Germany and all of Western civilization.

Stalin took a terrific beating at first. Between June, 1941, and March, 1942, he lost three million soldiers as the Nazi war machine rolled into Russia. He screamed for Allied aid, in spite of the fact he had so recently aided the Axis, and got it, largely from the U.S. lend-lease program. This debt was never repaid except by animosity. Lend-lease, plus the bravery the Russian people have shown in fighting for their country, made the world safe for the Kremlin gang.

Stalin, frankly, played us for suckers. He would promise anything we wanted to take place after the war—and did, at Teheran, Yalta and Potsdam. He kept us out of Turkey and the Balkans with his demands for a second front on Europe's other coasts, wanting to be sure his way with the Iron Curtain countries would not be impeded when we had defeated the Germans. He delayed taking action against Japan until the last possible moment, and did it then only when the Japanese couldn't resist and it served his purpose to move into Manchuria and reap the benefits of the Pacific war we had won.

As a matter of fact, Stalin had had a share in enabling the Japanese to attack us in 1941, by signing a non-agression pact that let them reduce their Manchurian forces.

What should we have done about Russia in World War II?

Well, a great many people felt, during the war, that we would have been far better advised if we had permitted the Nazis and the Reds to exhaust each other. No one, not even Napoleon, has ever invaded Russia successfully in more or less modern times—the country is too vast. We could have stepped in at the first sign that Hitler's armies were *not* bogging down. They were badly over-extended even in 1942. The Germans had an enormous supply problem. They might have overrun Russia more than they did, but they could never have sustained their conquest, especially as their air power diminished.

As it was, American lend-lease aid prevented Hitler from destroying the Red leadership, and forestalled what could have been a most salutary change in Russian government.

Our most serious error, however, was in letting Stalin argue us out of a Balkan invasion. The route up the Danube River, through the Iron Gate of Roumania into Eastern Europe, has been used successfully by invaders since ancient times. We could have used it, after prying Rommel out of Africa. Instead we wasted our energy invading Sicily and Italy, which could have been sealed off from the aid and bypassed.

And so, as the war drew to a close in Europe, the Reds took over the Balkans — plus Hungary, what was left of Austria, Czechoslovakia, Poland and East Germany.

We even pulled out liberating forces back in places to accommodate Stalin.

In Russian seizure of all the Iron Curtain countries, first force was necessary—the presence of Soviet troops. Next, a "coalition" government was formed, ostensibly under the control of popular leaders but with Soviet-designated Quislings in charge of the key ministries, notably the police and the judiciary. Elections were scheduled but only when the Communists might be sure they would win them—by instituting a police terror, by striking names from ballots beforehand, by imprisoning or liquidating opponents. Meanwhile, the people of the victim territory were intimidated by the massing of Soviet troops on their frontiers.

And, the "free" elections won, a People's Democracy established, there next followed the purging of any potential troublemakers the Communists might have missed, or any of their own number they wanted to be rid of, usually by the simple expedient of legal murder, since Communists possessed control of the courts and jury trial had been abolished.

That is how the U.S.S.R. built the Iron Curtain around East Germany, and Poland, and Hungary, Czechoslovakia, Bulgaria and Roumania—by force, enslaving the people and sending their leaders to concentration camps or to firing squads, brainwashing, torture, or whatever punishment the perverse mind of man could invent. There was a bit of a slip-up with regard to Yugoslavia and that maverick, Tito. This has annoyed the totalitarians ever since. Their seizure of Albania has only partly made up for it.

Stalin died or was murdered—who knows?—in 1953. It may be that an epoch ended then.

For almost three years a behind-the-scenes struggle for power went on among Soviet leaders. Significantly, it was marked by only one important killing, that of Stalin's hatchet man, the secret police chief, Lavrenti Beria. He had to go before the others, all about equal in stature, could feel safe.

Finally Nikita Khrushchev began to emerge as one of the more important contestants. In 1956 he treated the world to an astounding spectacle when he destroyed the image Russians held of a sainted

Stalin by denouncing the dead god-emperor as a bloodthirsty megalo-maniac at the 20th Party Congress.

This took courage. Yet Khrushchev and the others had not re-nounced Stalinism. When, later in the year, the Hungarian people rose in spontaneous protest against Russia, the rebellion was crushed with all of Stalin's treachery and ferocity. An overwhelming force of Soviet troops and tanks earned Khrushchev a new name, the Butcher of Budapest, to add to his earlier appellation, the Hangman of the Ukraine.

Khrushchev doesn't like to be called these names nowadays. He may feel he should receive credit for the comparative mercy he dealt out to demoted Stalinist rivals—Malenkov, Molotov and Kaganovich —and to Marshal Zhukov, whose influence in the Army he could not tolerate, and to goateed Bulganin, whom he at last no longer needed to front with him.

I have the feeling that Khrushchev is still something of a front man himself. That he has not yet, and may never fully inherit Stalin's mantle, despite his bull-roaring claim to our labor leaders in San Francisco that "I am the dictator of the working class! I will determine how well they eat!"

Not that we should be tempted to write off Mr. K. in any way. He is a highly intelligent man, and his intelligence may have taught him lessons about what happens to would-be world conquerors when they come up against a powerful people with a will for freedom. We shall see.

Meanwhile, I feel that Khrushchev is a man in something of a dilemma and that he realizes it.

When Stalin exploited his World War II victory by turning Russia into a colonial power, he took a tiger by the tail. He committed Russia to a policy that is in direct opposition to a rising tide of nationalism in the world. Peoples everywhere are demanding self-determination, the right to guide their own national destinies. The British, those pragmatic politicians, took cognizance of this irresistible movement and dismembered their weakened empire. But not Stalin.

His megalomania had to be fed, and he thus passed on to the Kremlin gang an insoluble problem. They can't even begin to let go of the tiger's tail—by loosening their grip on the Iron Curtain coun-tries, for instance — without encouraging revolt among peoples who hate Russia bitterly and will never be satisfied until her threat to them is ended.

Nor can the Russian leaders abandon their drive for world conquest. The Leninist-Marxist line demands a revolution of the world's workers, and no matter how this had been subverted into an instrument for more nationalist expansion, they are stuck with it. They can never let their supporting ideology — the totalitarian religion — be torn away. Otherwise they will stand exposed for exactly what they are, international bandits. Moreover, it is historical fact that when a dictatorship falters, it is soon overthrown.

Will the Russian people let themselves be led on a course of permanent expansion?

That's another Kremlin headache. The situation is aptly summed up in a pungent statement by Raymond Moley, who wrote in *Newsweek* for August 17, 1959: "Most amazing is the fact that the Soviet leaders [have] misjudged their own people. After forty years of discipline and brainwashing, those people are still concerned with products rather than propaganda, with good dinners rather than dialectic, with furniture rather than formulas, with kitchens rather than Khrushchev, and with freedom rather than fetishes." Yes, the Russians are human, too.

Even the new class, the eight million Party members who rule the nation's other two hundred million, would like their standard of living raised. And they, like other Russians and all the rest of the world, are scared to death of atomic war.

Is it any wonder that the words "peace and friendship" evoke cheers from Russians when they are spoken by visiting Americans? America has been painted in such threatening colors by Kremlin propagandists that just that simple phrase is vastly heartening. Most Russians suspect the Kremlin has lied to them — but how much is lies, and how much is truth?

We can live with Communism for a while. We have a better economic system, as has been amply demonstrated. Can the Reds live with us? We can only wait and see, and be ever on our guard that they do not expand in small political and military pushes that erode the resistance of underdeveloped countries, so as to gather more of them into the Communist camp.

In Russia, they went from the oppression of Feudalism to the oppression of Communism, with little of Capitalism in between. In the Western democracies we have gone from Feudalism to Freedom, with an increasingly liberal Capitalism the catalyst in a truly democratic process of evolution—and it is becoming difficult for Red propagandists to depict us as imperialists when their own system is so imperial.

Our problem is to demonstrate to neutral nations that their greatest danger lies in Communist penetration. We know that the Soviet expression of the Totalitarian Idea is running against the tide of history, and that the peoples of the world want freedom, not dictatorship; not colonial rule, but self-determination.

VI

COMMUNISM IN ASIA

Much of western feeling about the Chinese to this day may be summed up by an old jingle of Bret Harte's:

> ". . . and for ways that are dark
> And for tricks that are vain
> The heathen Chinee is peculiar."

I like Harte's stuff. He wrote stories of the California my grandfather knew as a Forty-niner, and I've read him since I was a boy—but he misjudged the Chinese. They may think in terms that differ from ours, but they are a very human and, in many respects, a magnificent people. They have been greatly wronged, particularly of late years. When my wife and I visited Hongkong in 1959 and stayed at a hotel about four miles from Red China, it was easy to imagine you could actually hear the sounds of their suffering.

The Communists have been supreme in China only for the past decade, yet they have already succeeded in forcibly changing a pattern of life which has existed for thousands of years. The majority of Chinese, however poor, used to enjoy a certain independence on the land they farmed. That's gone now. The family has always been the keystone of Chinese culture—and the Reds are in the process of abolishing families, separating husbands and wives, parents and children.

A few years ago they made an official hero of a teen-age boy who betrayed 281 people, including his own father, to the Party police. They are deliberately infecting children with hate. Adults may groan at hideously long hours in fields and factories on a diet close to the starvation level, they may even rebel, singly or in small groups. Children, seduced by somewhat better rations in the communal kitchens, swallow propaganda with their food. The Communists are building their strength in the rising generation.

The favorite theme of Red Chinese propaganda is hatred of America and Americans. The way we're portrayed, you'd think a fanged Uncle Sam ate Chinese kids for breakfast. The motive is obvious—our country stands as a barrier to Communist expansion. But when you get close to it, as we did in Hongkong, it's really chilling.

Yes, Hongkong last year was quite an experience. A fascinating

51

city, bustling and colorful, crammed with hundreds of thousands of
refugees—the lucky ones. The British crown colony copes as it can
with the housing problem; many still live in shacks. However, Western
vision and energy have provided employment for the displaced. Hongkong's busy commerce reveals what modern Asia might become with
freedom.

Our idea of freedom is quite foreign to Asia, however. At a Hongkong
luncheon, I sat next to a newspaper publisher from Calcutta, a highly
educated, informed Indian. I was shocked that his paper's circulation
amounted only to 100,000 in a city of seven million. He was thoroughly
annoyed that *Time* had printed a story about Calcutta which he felt
was derogatory of the city and of Indian leaders. I tried to explain to
him that *Time* did not necessarily reflect the feeling of the American
people nor of our government, and suggested that his paper might well
tell its readers about the workings of our free press.

How well this went over, I don't know. It occurred to me that, while
we were talking, the grim threat of Red China overhung us all, so
short a distance away.

The situation becomes doubly tragic when you think that the
Western world has had so much to do with making the Communist
conquest of China possible. How much a little vision and energy,
properly applied, could have accomplished a mere twenty-five or
thirty years ago! There might have been no Red China today.

But then, Western nations have been bungling relations with
the Chinese for the last century or more.

China is one of the most ancient of civilized countries. The Chinese
had a fairly advanced culture when the ancestors of some Americans
were running around in animal skins and worshipping trees. Con-
fucius, who fathered Chinese philosophy, uttered his maxims five
hundred years before Christ. But China's history ran apart from
that of Europe until quite recent times.

In the very old days, some Chinese goods—incense, silks and other
luxuries—reached Europe by caravan through Central Asia and
the Middle East. By the sixteenth and seventeenth centuries a
seaborne commerce with Europeans had begun, though confined to
one port, Canton. The Chinese felt with some justification that
the outer world was peopled by barbarians, and they shut their
doors to other nations.

Europe's expansionism could not be denied, however, and in 1840-42
the English provoked and waged the Opium War, to open a market

for the drug grown in their colony, India. The rights and wrongs of this maneuver—the wrongs not all on the side of Britain—will probably be argued forever. From the standpoint of history, China's closed doors were gradually forced open to Western trade, and the Chinese people slowly awakened to the fact that if they weren't to be exploited forever in the modern world they had better adapt to Western modes and methods. The world marches, whether you like it or not.

Revolution against the corrupt imperial Manchu dynasty broke out in 1911. But China's revolutionists were amateurs. They wanted a republic, without understanding the workings of a republic, or its politics. Even Dr. Sun Yat-sen, the idealist who became the Father of the Revolution, didn't really know what he was doing. After years of tumult in China, he noted the success of the Russian Bolsheviks with envy, and asked for Communist political and military advisers to help him reorganize his party, the Kuomintang, and create an army for the pacification of the country. He also invited the fledgling Chinese Communist Party to merge with the KMT.

Dr. Sun died in 1925, and Chiang Kai-shek inherited a mare's nest of political intrigue and a nation torn apart by war lords. Chiang used the Russian-trained forces at his command to crush some of these military racketeers, made alliances with others, and finally united China to some extent—after he had expelled the Communists from the KMT and outlawed them. This man *did* know what he was doing.

But the Kuomintang was never the instrument it could have been. Nor did Chiang ever quite succeed in destroying the Chinese Communists who, with Russian help, survived. Mao Tse-tung led the ragged Red horde on a retreat to the far northwest, his main purpose to outlast Chiang and the KMT. For the Japanese had begun their attempt to conquer China in 1937, an effort that continued through World War II. Mao occasionally fought the common enemy, but only as it served Red interests.

War's end in 1945 found Chiang in a perilous position. His party was shot through with corruption, the country exhausted by so many years of fighting. Inflation was rampant.

Mao's Communists, on the other hand, had emerged from the conflict considerably strengthened. The Kuomintang held the cities, by and large, but the Reds had much of rural China. Civil war promptly burst out after the Japanese surrendered.

The United States tried to intervene. But we failed to understand either the Chinese or the issues at stake, and our impractical demand that Chiang's Nationalists and Mao's so-called 'agrarian reformers' join in a coalition government was rebuffed by both sides. We withdrew and, in disgust, stopped supplying the Nationalists for a year and a half. During this period Russia never ceased supporting the Reds. It's a wonder Chiang held out as long as he did.

Our abandonment of him cost him heavily at home. Many influential Chinese were already sick of Kuomintang venality, which Chiang could not control. By contrast the Communists appeared to be dedicated and honest. Besides, Mao himself had promised a very gradual change toward a New Democracy which, though socialistic, did not sound impossible to live with.

By the time we came to our senses and resumed helping Chiang once more, almost all noncombatant Chinese had turned neutral in the civil war. It was too late to save Chiang, or China. In 1949 our luckless and gallant friend, with his crumbling Nationalist forces, was harried out of his country to Formosa, where we have had to defend him ever since.

The Communists completed taking over the mainland.

The Chinese people quickly found that the People's Republic—Mao's euphemism for his dictatorship—had no intention whatever of implementing Mao's blue-sky promises.

The New Democracy simply didn't happen. Tight political control was imposed from Peking as a prelude to the gigantic tasks of reconstruction. To create an effective policing organization, Communist Party membership was rapidly increased by several millions—and the rest of the stunned nation put under the thumb of myriad spies and petty enforcers to insure conformity to the totalitarian way of life. For the moment farm land was redistributed among agricultural workers, landlords in general being liquidated. Personal assets, however—especially savings—were extorted from the entire population. The Reds badly needed money; where they came on it, they took it. Chinese businesses, as well as foreign, were seized.

Another money-making device the Reds employed is worth noting. They vastly increased production of opium and heroin, for smuggling to every corner of the free world. Addiction to narcotics has multiplied as a result, in the U.S. particularly. It is dollar exchange the Reds most desire.

Thus, unfortunate Americans are contributing a portion of the financing for expansion of current Chinese industry, which has been nothing short of phenomenal.

New railroads, power dams, steel mills and factory complexes have been appearing at an increasing rate all over China, and there is no sign of a let-up according to recent reports. The country has the potential of becoming the world's ranking power, with its more than six hundred and fifty million people.

Mao Tse-tung's most pressing problem is feeding this enormous population. In 1955, spurred by falling production on the number-less tiny farms created by his land redistribution, he began to collectivize agriculture. Though food yields have been stepped up in some years since, this is a highly unpopular program—and a dangerous one for the Communists. In time of war, five hundred million disaffected peasants could bring disaster down on Red China.

Khrushchev must have had such a possibility in mind when he criticized Mao's rigid system of rural communes. Certainly the Chinese propensity for making war currently worries the Russians—which is something they brought on themselves.

China's war-like attitude stems from the Korean War, in its beginnings strictly a Russian adventure. As it has a bearing on present Sino-Soviet relations, let's talk about it.

North Korea was a Russian satellite in 1950. Encouraged by a U.S. statement of policy that indicated we had lost interest in the fate of South Korea, the Soviets caused their puppet government to invade the lower half of the peninsula. They could threaten Japan very nicely from South Korea. But the U.S. reconsidered, as we all know, the United Nations came in on the fracas, and the North Koreans, after an initial success, began to take a beating. If Russia entered the war openly, a world conflict might result. The Red Chinese found a way out of the dilemma.

They couldn't declare war against the U.N. lest they spoil their chances of ever gaining membership in the organization, but they could and did send huge numbers of "volunteers" to the aid of the North Koreans. A stalemate ensued at the center of the shattered little country.

Nobody won the Korean War. The Chinese came out of it with more gain than other contestants, however. Though they got a black eye when thousands of their volunteers, captured, preferred being sent to Chiang on Formosa to going home, their troops as a whole *had* stopped the powerful U.N. war machine. And, in redeeming a Russian failure, they had climbed closer to parity with the Soviets.

North Korea is more a Chinese than a Russian satellite now, we hear. The Kremlin can hardly be happy about that, by and large.

But are there grounds for the western hope of a real conflict of interest between Russia and China?

Well, the Chinese definitely assumed the Russian role when they squeezed the French out of Indo-China. The Communist Vietnamese were their boys, and China supplied them. It was Peking's Chou En-lai, also, who won international acceptance of North Vietnam in the Korea-type settlement at Geneva.

China has made her influence felt in Russia's relations with the Iron Curtain countries. When Poland became restive following the Hungarian revolt in 1956, Peking may have saved the U.S.S.R. embarrassment by threatening pressure against any Communist country trying to get out from under Moscow's domination, but in itself this successful gesture was a challenge of Kremlin authority.

The Chinese have interefered in the Middle East and Africa. They have sent factories to Yemen, they have an active embassy in Iraq and they have supplied arms to the Algerian rebels.

Since Stalin's death, Mao Tse-tung has set himself up as an interpreter of the International Communist line. This must infuriate Khrushchev, who is trying to soften the doctrine. What really gives the Russians pause these days, if we read the news aright, is the reckless way Mao is demonstrating the inherent violence of Communism in Asia.

China will likely continue her propaganda attacks on the U.S.A. and the West, and her war-like adventures in Asia. Mao can keep the Chinese people united only by keeping them afraid of America, and he has to keep the rest of Asia off balance in order to forestall moves against China. In Asia, force is the key to power. Mao needs victories, even small ones, to offset China's internal troubles.

In 1959 his regime was forced to admit that production goals had not been met. There are reports of disaffection within the Chinese Communist Party and the Army; purges have become necessary. Minorities in China's West are supposedly in rebellion. The summer of 1959 was one of droughts and floods, so old man famine has turned up again.

We would be in error, however, to take comfort from the troubles of the Red Chinese. There is as yet no sign that their power has been, or can be seriously challenged inside China. In the present world situation we cannot challenge them—not without taking on Russia as well.

My wife and I went to Japan from Hongkong. You may find our observations interesting.

First of all, there is a difference between the Chinese we met in Hongkong and the Japanese. The Chinese seem to admire Americans but do not respect us; the Japanese respect us, but do not admire us. The usual American reaction is superficial: we assume that the Japanese felt the weight of our Armed Forces, hence the respect; the Chinese were our allies in World War II and we won, hence the admiration. However, it goes deeper.

Chinese culture has been under assault since the turn of the century and has been weakened. Japanese culture, despite a military defeat for the nation, has been well preserved, and is valid and valuable for its people. Changes in method are afoot in Japan. There are few changes in manner.

We can learn much from the Japanese, a people who succeeded in taking what they wished from European and Western life and yet maintained their own integrity. We must remember that much of Japanese culture came from China and the soul of the Oriental peoples is indivisible.

The Japanese worship beauty in rocks, trees and woods. Their cities often reflect Western ugliness, as do their industrial establishments. However, the villages are beautiful—every village a garden and each street a vista.

The way the economy has revived is miraculous. The Japanese, like the Germans, have made the most of our aid. Their giant strides are evident in the building going on. In many cases their modern hotels and office buildings are superior to ours. However, it is in the field of precision work such as cameras, binoculars and microscopes that the re-orientation of industry is most noticeable. These products are second to none. Low prices at which they sell in export markets are due, not so much to low labor costs as to volume of output.

True, Japan still makes substandard merchandise. It is my feeling that the Government should discourage such exports. The country will do better on equality levels and encounter less discrimination in the foreign markets.

It is worth noting that taxes on Japanese corporations are ten per cent lower than ours, which helps bring out venture capital. The Japanese are venturesome; they must be, because the country lives on its exports.

Our own industry will increasingly have to compete with Japanese goods, and we can do it by holding wages, cutting profits, overhead and taxes, and by selling more. In any case, we need the Japanese in Asia as much as they need us. The cooperation of our two nations is imperative if the Asian standard of living, outside Red China, is to be raised to levels where Communism is no longer attractive as the last desperate remedy for discouraged and depressed peoples.

Japan is as alert as we are to the dangers of Communism. The Japanese live next door to Russia and China. Japanese Communists, even Socialists, are all but impotent, if noisy.

There is one thing Americans traveling in Japan can do; drop that attitude of superiority! Try to understand. Actually, in some ways we are inferior to the Japanese. In our national culture and in energy, we do not even begin to come up to this remarkable people. We have know-how, perhaps, but they have, in their innermost spirit, know-why.

The Japanese have problems—and one of them is how to feed the people from the acres they have in cultivation. They can't do it, even with their great skill. This is an all-Asian, all-world problem.

VII

WORLD PROBLEMS OF THE U.S.A.

It isn't easy for a nation like ours to face up to the responsibilities of world leadership. Any leader must exercise a judicious amount of domination, and we don't like to dominate other peoples. Until we had fought two wars against the British government—our Revolution for political freedom, the War of 1812 for commercial freedom—we ourselves were dominated. We remember that quite vividly.

Nor do we care much for the method Britain used to keep her position in the world—the maintenance of a "balance of power"—during her long period of leadership. There is too much of coercion in it for our taste. We would infinitely prefer to secure the cooperation of other nations, to work with them democratically toward mutual goals of betterment.

But the balance of power era is not yet ended. True, the world situation has changed radically since the days of British-enforced peace. But here we are, pitted against the Soviet Union as the richest and strongest of the democracies, and the Soviets have no faith at all in the international democracy we would like to see operating.

What is Khrushchev trying to do but set up a balance of power—temporarily, at least—between Russia and the United States? And if the Russians insist on bypassing the United Nations in this reactionary manner, we shall probably have to compromise to some extent if we are to deal with them.

As a matter of fact, in negotiating "summit" meetings we are already compromising. But we must do what we can in a period of transition, without losing sight of our ultimate obligation to international democracy and a peaceful world.

And isn't it true that the historical balances of power had an element of service in them? That they were maintained not only by strength, but by the exercising of leadership and responsibility?

Many may answer that such leadership was seized by force, by intimidation, or because no other force could combat it, and hence was morally wrong. But the facts disprove, in part, such a conclusion. While Britain, in particular, dominated much of the earth until recent times, she also ruled over world trade, with resultant benefits to the people involved. It is true that the British people benefited more than the dominated in the achievement of wealth and prosperity, but you can't ignore the aid extended to British colonies, or the fact that trade and exports enabled them to improve their way of life.

Other European powers exploited their colonies much more ruthlessly than did Britain. The colonial system was far from perfect. But it worked, in its time. Now conditions are changed—but only partly changed. Witness the treatment that Russia accords her satellites.

The Europeans incurred a great deal of enmity among peoples they colonized. Indeed, all strong nations have come to be regarded with suspicion — and the U.S. is tarred with the same brush. Our own commercial policies with regard to poorer countries have not always been fair or enlightened; we have done our share of exploiting in the past. And nowadays the Communists busily propagandize us as "dollar imperialists," taking care not to explain what they mean by that phrase. Is any country trying to develop international trade imperialistic?

That Russia seems to be less suspect than the U.S. in this matter may stem from the fact that the Soviets haven't yet caught up with us industrially. The small nations that have tried trading with the Soviets have learned something about these "ruble imperialists," however.

Another element enters into it. We are richer than anybody else, and this stirs a natural human envy in other peoples. No matter how much we do for them, they're not going to like us, really. We could take lessons from the English here. In their heyday, they never expected to be liked. But they knew that the world respects strength that is wisely used, and admires a strong nation that has a sound policy regarding its international relations, and sticks to it. That is where we have fallen down—we have vacillated in our policy.

A little analysis of recent world history proves it.

With World War I, Britain went into a decline. As the least damaged power among the victors, the U.S. was in a position to assume leadership, and President Wilson did his best to bring the new League of Nations into being so that there might be international democracy on this earth.

He may have been ahead of his time; certainly he was ahead of world feeling. Between the politicians of Europe and the U.S. Senate, Wilson was scuttled. We repudiated his League, retreated into an unreal isolationism, and earned a reputation for irresponsibility among other nations.

Inevitably, as a result of our withdrawal and the unwillingness of Europe to halt Hitler and Stalin without definite assurances of our support, World War II developed.

Once more, we emerged as the least damaged victor, and this time world leadership was ours whether we wanted it or not. No other nation except the Soviet Union could even think of assuming the role. Meanwhile, the Soviets had already begun a program aimed at world conquest. We disarmed — though we did launch a counter-program for the economic rehabilitation of Europe and other sick areas, through the Marshall Plan.

We awakened to our real responsibilities with the Korean War. But by this time International Communism possessed a vitality it would never have had except for our reluctance to recognize it for what it was and is—the enemy.

The Cold War began. All the world afraid of a hot one, but the lines of battle drawn nevertheless.

We do have some advantages, though we do not seem to have made the most of them.

We are not, and have never been, an imperial power. We have added very little to our continental territory. The Panama Canal Zone is leased by us. In the case of Puerto Rico, the people strongly desired inclusion, and they enjoy full citizenship as well as all the economic benefits of our democracy. Alaska and Hawaii long clamored for statehood, and have finally achieved it. In the Philippine Islands, the people desired independence and they got it—plus continuing economic support. Our record, as opposed to Russia's and China's, should be apparent.

Our extension of foreign aid is unparalleled in history; no other nation has ever been so generous. Since World War II we have shelled out more than seventy-five billion dollars to other countries, and much of it has small chance of ever being repaid. To the Marshall Plan, now completed, the free world owes its present economic health. Has any country other than the United States ever been so assiduous in building up commercial rivals?

Some Americans have criticized our foreign aid program for this very reason. But our free world competitors in commerce are also our allies in the cold war, and by making them self-supporting we strengthen ourselves. As well, they are now realizing their responsibilities toward us, and are lowering barriers to U.S. goods, since they have got on their feet. The ideal of a free world with free world trade is probably unattainable so long as the world remains divided between free and slave peoples, but at least we can lead the way toward commercial freedom on our half of the globe.

There is, also, evidence of a gradual but massive shift of world opinion in favor of our motives and those of the West in the last year or so, a shift that has been accelerated in Asia by the aggressive threat of China.

We must learn to live with the mulishness of others, and the lingering distrust that is the lot of a world leader.

For instance, in Europe many people dislike our dominance in NATO—the North Atlantic Treaty alliance. But neither do they like our recent suggestions that the European countries should carry more of the burden of Western defenses. If we were to pull back our troops and dismantle our plane and missile bases, however, there would be a vast outcry that we were returning to isolationism, and appeasing Khrushchev.

These are the challenges a nation incurs in becoming a world leader. You say it isn't worth it! We can't get out from under the load. Isolation isn't possible any more. The world has grown too small. If we should attempt to withdraw, to create a "fortress America," we would simply be forcing the rest of the world into the Communist orbit—and making ourselves a target.

Can this country, *will* this country, preserve the freedoms we have inherited, by extending the strength of democracy to underdeveloped peoples? Can we maintain the position of strength formerly exercised by Western Europe in a balance-of-power situation, and at the same time press on toward world-wide liberty?

It is largely up to us, the ordinary people of these United States. Each one of us must endeavor to understand what goes on beyond our borders if our government is to have the knowledgeable support it requires. This country must succeed. Our allies will not stay with us very long if we begin losing. That, too, is one of the penalties of leadership.

Helping other countries is a tough job. Witness our experience with the Marshall Plan. It was often wasteful, on occasion badly administered, and it was poorly received by some nations benefiting. However, there will always be differences of theory between the recipients of aid and our administrators; human error is bound to occur, and there will be political pressures influencing decisions, as ever.

But we're committed to a policy of helping other countries now—and we should do so, insofar as we can without wrecking ourselves. Which is another vital consideration.

First of all, we need to define our aim clearly: to combat Communism and promote international stability by raising the level of well-being among depressed peoples, but not to allow ourselves to be used in ways contrary to our interests.

Ultimately, the only way to relieve the distress of the backward millions of Asia and Africa is by free enterprise, new capital and new capitalists. Many of these peoples need to have pointed out to them that the poverty of small nations, very often, is due to expropriation, discriminatory taxing of foreign enterprises, or foreign exchange control that prevents investment of outside capital, while their domestic policies hamper accumulation of capital within the country.

Let these conditions be corrected by existing governments, and capital will arrive or be raised quickly enough. Venture capital anticipates reasonable profits, according to the risk involved. If risk exceeds the expectation of profit, capital stays home, or lies idle in the vault.

Let these people be shown, also, that their poverty provides fallow ground for the seed of Communism, and that Communism means colonization and exploitation. It is nonsense to blame the capitalistic nations of the West for their plight. If it were not for the West they would still be two centuries behind the times, and worse off than they are now.

Meanwhile, there are two main fields where the West can furnish relief: in food supply, and in health programs. Until these nations can feed themselves properly, countries with food surpluses should export them where they will do the most good, at prices the needy can afford to pay or on long-term credits. The United Nations health program should be expanded, and other philanthropic programs gathered under its aegis for greater efficiency. Hundreds of hospitals could be built with the labor of the countries involved, and staffed with native doctors trained to cope with prevalent diseases. Such an international health service would cost little, compared to the billions already spent. Healthy people are productive people.

The U.S. in particular could gain much by insistence on working through the United Nations. The little fellows in the organization are actively beginning to resent the dominance of the major powers. There is even fear that the U.N. may suffer the fate of the League of Nations —a tragedy we must bend every effort to avoid.

True, the Russians are largely to blame for undermining U.N. authority, with their constant exercise of veto power in the Security Council, but this country also has been forced to adopt certain pressures and political expedients. We are treading a delicate path between balance-of-power policy and international democratic processes.

Let us emphasize our aims in the U.N., stress that we are not striving for world dominance but for world democracy and world freedom. And, by combining words with deeds, let us secure the understanding and cooperation of smaller nations.

Words are important. A basic problem in our relations with others —one we haven't solved well so far—is that of explaining ourselves to others. It could be that we need to understand our own ideology better.

We are considered materialistic by the world at large, probably because of our outspoken devotion to the political and economic aspects of our system. We insist that these very material conditions permit our concept of the individual dignity and freedom of man to flourish.

But what do we mean by "the individual dignity and freedom of man?"

We believe, first and foremost, that the individual man or woman is important, in himself and herself. Each individual is possessed of a human spirit that is distinct in itself and unlike any other.

We believe that each individual has the right to work out his own destiny within the fabric of our society. This does not mean that the individual has the right to fling principle to the wind and enjoy himself at the expense of others. With rights go responsibilities. But we do believe—as was said by Theophilus Parsons, one of the founders of our nation—that personal liberty consists of "the right every man in the state has, to do whatever is not prohibited by laws, *to which he has given his consent.*"

We believe that consent to law may be given by a majority of our free people, and that the majority rules. This may curtail the liberty of some, but law there must be, and if it is an expression of majority wish it is more apt to be fair for all the people.

We believe that other peoples should be free to choose their own way of life. We do *not* believe that our concepts or our system can or should be imposed anywhere else in the world. We have what we feel is best for us, at our present stage of development. Others may disagree that it is best for them, and we believe that they ought to know what is best for them.

For instance, in Japan it is feared that so much individual liberty may prove disruptive in the family group. But if, as in Japan, individuals wish to merge their liberties in a family group, so that the group in effect becomes the individual, who is to say them nay? Is this not the wish of the majority?

We believe that freedom, in whatever measure it may be desired, is the right of all peoples everywhere, and it is our wish that they may achieve it—in their own way, and in their own time.

This, I believe, is what we mean by our concept of the individual dignity and freedom of man.

Most Americans live by a rather practical code. We believe that a man should be judged by his record—what he does, not by how he explains himself. That his value depends on his ability to produce—we're a nation of workers. That security lies within the individual—if you've got the stuff, you'll make out all right. That a right-headed man deals fairly with others—honesty being the best policy. That co-operation is the way to get things done—in union there is strength, all the way down the line.

In other words, let each man achieve for himself what his character, talent and ambition will allow, working with others as this is possible, and honoring the basic rights of humanity where anybody else is concerned.

By and large, this attitude is reflected in our foreign policy. The trouble is we haven't made it plain enough.

Official diplomacy can't win this battle. The State Department is doing a better job than it has in the past, but it and such communications agencies as the U.S. Information Service and the Voice of America are not adequate. We could use more experienced commercial attaches in consulates, men trained to advance our ideological as well as our business interests; this would help even at the embassy level. The people who could do the most good, however, are Americans doing business in foreign lands.

When Dr. Malik was President of the U.N. General Assembly, he called on American business men to serve as ambassadors for the West when he spoke to the Harvard Graduate School of Business Administration on its fiftieth anniversary. They needed, he said, to become more versatile, to help prove our gift to humanity as well as our material achievements. He was so right.

Business is not only the foundation of our society, it is our main contact with the world. Education in the fundamentals of Americanism is necessary at all levels, but business men especially should have a firm grounding in international relations, geopolitics, philosophy and comparative culture, if they are to be effective representatives of America. They can add to, and better the job performed by diplomats. How can the American motive be better put forth than as the philosophy underlying a business deal of mutual benefit? But our business-

men, as Malik said, need to understand the people they are dealing
with, too, the more ably to interpret us, and the more ably to interpret
foreign peoples to us here at home.

President Eisenhower has called for more "people-to-people" contacts. A distinguished merchant, J. C. Penney, has said: "The great
principles we have inherited from the world's experience are not statements to be read occasionally. They are actual forces to be directed
upon whatever we do every day as our job. We work with the forces.
But they work for us!"

Let every American who goes abroad anywhere try to reflect our
standards, our beliefs, in the simple matter of personal behavior. Many
of us fling our weight around, are loud, boisterous, demanding. This
doesn't go down very well with our hosts. They expect guests to act
decently, and why shouldn't they? Their ways are merely different
from ours. Remember: we need them, as they need us.

In the last few years the Russians have launched a great commercial offensive against us. They have proclaimed with fanfare that
whatever we can do they can do better, either in foreign aid *or*
commerce.

It may be some comfort to know that they have been guilty of
wastes and blunders, too. They sent 4,000 jeeps to Indonesia in 1958
—vehicles that went to pieces in the tropical heat. A Soviet team
failed to cope with a South Asian flood, unable to get a decision from
Moscow while the victims suffered—and the U.S.S.R. got a black eye.
Tons of Soviet cement became worthless in Burmese humidity. The
Russians bought rice in Burma — and sold it to Burma's usual customers.

Yes, the Russians make their own mistakes. But take no comfort
from their foreign trade shenanigans.

They have an advantage here, in that they can manipulate trade
in ways we cannot. With their totalitarian economy, everything state-
owned, they can enter into what amounts to barter arrangements,
exchanging their products for those of another country. For political
ends, they can juggle markets, using subsidies and credits if necessary,
since they have a vast latitude on costs—their underpaid labor gives
them a tremendous edge. They can undersell at will, make another
country dependent on their trade, then jack up their prices. To the
Russians, prices do not have the same meaning they do under our
competitive economy; an end product is worth what it is convenient
for them to charge.

We have to compete against this sort of thing in the world market, and it's rough. But it isn't impossible.

In the first place, we should show tempted nations what it means to trade with the U.S.S.R., in the light of what has happened to others. Nasser's Egypt has been flooded with "technicians"—agitators, that is —who constitute a knotty problem, and the country has to a large extent lost control of her vitally important cotton exports. Finland, defeated by Russia in World War II, had no chance of resisting Soviet commercial imperialism—and now her economy is tied so tightly to Russia's that she might almost be a satellite.

On the positive side, there are a number of ways in which we can improve our competitive position.

We can work harder to lower barriers to trade in the free world. There are some hard-held opinions about tariffs and trade, and it will not be easy to break down prejudices either in our own country or abroad. On the continent of Europe the Common Market shared by Italy, France, West Germany and the Benelux countries is a step in the right direction, especially as it aims towards a United States of Europe. But it has a rival in the British-led Free Trade Area, a measure more or less of self-defense for England, the Scandinavian countries, Portugal, Switzerland and Austria. A trade war between the two blocs could split Europe commercially—to the detriment of all concerned—and furthermore cause discrimination against American exports. Here is a great opportunity for leadership by this country. Indeed, we *must* convince our European allies that cooperation is essential, and that the best hope for the future we all share lies in freer trade relations throughout the Atlantic community, including the U.S.A.

This done, a policy of free trade for all nations outside the Communist sphere should follow. Free peoples can contribute most to each other through mutual commerce, without curbs that hinder productiveness. If exploitation is feared, let machinery be set up to arbitrate differences, if possible within the United Nations. Such a step toward commercial democracy could lead so effectively towards one world— and international political democracy.

A strategy commission composed of men from U.S. business and labor could do a lot toward formulating a coordinated "trade plan" for this country. Our labor unions have already performed very ably in combatting the subversive activities of the Soviets' world-wide labor network. But let their leaders now expand their horizons, and aid in actively promoting U.S. world trade. Only trade can raise the standard of living of workers in other parts of the world, and unless standards elsewhere come up, we cannot expect to maintain our own high wage levels.

We are doing quite well in the field of development aid extended through world financial institutions, to which we have contributed most of the capital—the World Bank, the Export-Import Bank, the Development Loan Fund. But we should make sure that such loans are beneficial to our labor and to free world labor. Likewise, the trade agreements we make as a nation should insure against exploitation of labor abroad.

As for the three or four billions we provide yearly to our allies, it is high time that such aid be reduced except for emergencies. Secretary of the Treasury Anderson has been outspoken on this subject, and in demanding that we get more help in furnishing developmental capital to the world. Europe may protest, but from the standpoint of pure self-interest we could better spend our money on subsidies of exports to put our products in a competitive position with Soviet products. Certainly we should extend economic aid only where our products are given reciprocal treatment in international trade.

Above all, in negotiating for trade, we should tell our customers and the free world *what we are doing and why we are doing it.* This is cold war, it isn't going to be over for a long time, probably, and we can only gain respect by stating our position in clear, unmistakable terms.

Now, how about the trade with Russia that Khrushchev is urging, along with his call for "peaceful competition?"

Whether we actually need anything Russia has to sell is perhaps beside the point. It is a little ridiculous that the Russians should expect us to trade on a basis of long-term credits, extended by us. Let us say, rather, that we should attach certain pre-conditions to trade with the Soviets.

We should demand that they and the Iron Curtain countries not only pay up their lend-lease bill, but what is outstanding on American properties and investments they confiscated. Perhaps these debts could be discharged by a system of credits on going trade, when established.

And, if we are to trade with Russia, it must be on a basis of honest reciprocity—none of their dumping of products to depress world markets, no secret deals with other countries taking unfair advantage. The Communists are old hands at that sort of thing. Let peaceful competition be trade that makes for true mutual benefit, "give and take," not just "take." Competition should never mean the destruction of either party in world commerce. Trade is not the continuation of the cold war by other means.

Khrushchev also urges trade with Red China, and he has renewed pressure for China's admission into the U.N.

Well, we might make a "trade" in this area—let China become a U.N. member in exchange for abolition of veto power in the Security Council. Decisions by a majority in the Council would be much more democratic. Not that China should be made a permanent member of the Council, by any means, or even be admitted to the Council at first. In fact, Red Chinese membership in the U.N. itself should be predicated on good behavior and a genuine manifestation of a will toward peace—no more Asian aggressions.

It may have occurred to you by this time that the Russians and the Chinese will not readily accept any of these pre-conditions. But they are points for negotiation, and they provide opportunity to proclaim our viewpoint to the world. Is there anything unfair in what we have set down?

Let it all be negotiated in the United Nations, with the world watching—and we will see who stands in the right.

Actually, it might be to Communist interests to find a realistic basis for co-existence, suitable to their own national objectives as well as ours. If they could only get over feeling the need to force their system on others! At bottom, this means they haven't the confidence necessary to enable them to compete with our system. And until some such revolution in Communist philosophy can occur, they must remain our enemies, unfortunately, and "co-existence" will be possible only as we maintain a position of strength and preparedness.

VIII

WORLD SORE SPOTS AND U.S.A. INTERESTS

For Americans a maddening thing about the cold war is that so many of its "battles" are fought in ways and places remote from us. And so often we can influence the outcome of these engagements only remotely, and sometimes not at all.

Take the national elections in Malaya in 1959. In this brand new democracy, made independent of Britain in 1957, an indigestible minority of Chinese who are subject to pressures from Red China control the nation's commerce. Fortunately the 1957 election was won by the party most friendly to the West. But there are over a million Chinese in Singapore, not yet part of the Malayan Federation but eager to join, and if that happens Malaya could flame with civil war. The situation would be made to order for the Communists, and we would find it very difficult to intervene.

Remember what happened in Laos. The Communists pulled back when that tiny country appealed to the United Nations for military aid and the West indicated that Chinese aggression might provoke another Korea. However, the Laotian story is far from ended. Laos furnishes a corridor into Thailand, Cambodia and Malaya.

It has been suggested that Communist strategy for the Far East is to unite the manpower of China with the industrial capacity of Japan and the natural resources of Southeast Asia and Indonesia. That may be.

But look at the map. With the big southeast Asian peninsula just mentioned in Chinese hands, Burma and India would be cut off to the east, and these countries, particularly India, are the key to the Asian situation.

India leads among the neutral Afro-Asian nations. India is making considerable progress with her industry and commerce and to some extent, agriculture. India is a showcase for the adaptation of western methods to Oriental uses by democratic process. As Walter Lippmann says, such a demonstration must be made in a big country like India, and succeed overwhelmingly if other uncommited nations of the world are to turn from the enticements of Communism.

On the other hand, if a despairing India does turn to Communism we will have lost the cold war and the West will be isolated, the far more numerous dark-skinned inhabitants of our planet set against us.

Prime Minister Nehru has had, in India, problems to shatter a lesser man. Not only has he had to build industry and correct injurious practices in food production, he has had to encourage democracy among a diverse population inadequately prepared, to educate backward masses toward political responsibility in an enervating climate that wore out most Europeans in a few years. And don't forget the pressure of India's exploding birth rate. Can you blame Nehru for trying to appease the Chinese, to gain a little time?

Now, with her sister countries of Burma, Bhutan, Nepal and Pakistan, India is hemmed in on the north by the aggressive Chinese all the way to Afghanistan, a nation the Russians have reduced almost to the status of a satellite by economic and military penetration.

The situation is rapidly deteriorating for not only these beleaguered Asian nations but for us. We have extended them a good deal of aid, especially Pakistan and India. Can we afford to lessen it, or is this an emergency in which we should increase the flow of aid? It will require eight to ten billion dollars, Lippmann estimates, to put India solidly on her feet within the next eight to fifteen years. This is our dilemma—where to find the money.

Meanwhile, India has her own dilemma. Does she dare to go to war with China—or can she refuse to fight, with a big gun pointing down her throat from the Himalayas? How much of her production can she divert to the sinews of war, without wrecking herself? Can she fight a war at all without western military aid? Will she bring on an atomic holocaust?

It is doubtful that Mao Tse-tung wants a full scale war; certainly Khrushchev doesn't. But they'd both like to see Nehru ousted in India. Not only is Nehru holding India together, he occupies a position in the Asian mind that Mao covets— that of paladin of all the oppressed Asian peoples.

We might remind ourselves that Nehru had his 71st birthday in 1960. And he seems a weary man.

The Middle East rivals India as a critical area. Historically a crossroads of the world, it has been a battleground for thousands of years. Many conquerors have met their defeat in the region—the ancient Egyptians, the Greeks, the Assyrians, the Romans, the Moslems, the Turks, and more recently France and Britain, who held mandates there.

Middle Eastern peoples have known little independence in their

turbulent history. The power of the last oppressors, the Turkish
Sultans, was broken as short a time ago as World War I. With freedom, there has come an upsurge of Arab nationalism. But while the
Turkish people have had a chance at establishing a stable democracy
in their own territory, and used it to good purpose, the various Arab
countries—Syria, Iraq, Jordan, Saudia Arabia, Yemen, and Egypt—
have lagged in developing progressively.

There are many reasons for this. Long periods of foreign domination have contributed to the lethargy of the people, poor leadership
and local autocracy haven't helped. Perhaps more to the point, Arabic
peoples are not especially homogeneous. City Arabs are very different
from country Arabs, many of whom are nomads and resent any re-
straint except the laws of ancient tribal tradition. And as there are
wide cultural gaps between urban and rural populations in all the
Middle Eastern states, so there are considerable differences in the
political aspirations of the states themselves.

Since the Egyptian Revolution of 1952 was taken over by President
Nasser—a somewhat autocratic character—he has vigorously preached
the cause of Pan-Arabism. Unfortunately this means, in his interpretation, Egyptian domination of an Arab empire reaching from the
Atlantic shoulder of Africa to the Persian Gulf. So far, Nasser has
persuaded only Syria to join with Egypt in the United Arab Republic
and not too many Syrians are pleased with the arrangement.

The vision of Arab unity does hold magic. But other Arab countries
cannot see surrendering sovereignty to the Egyptians. A few years
ago, in fact, six of them denounced or expelled Nasser's military
attaches for interfering in domestic matters. They had ground for
alarm. In 1958 Nasser did his best to turn the Iraq revolution into
an Egyptian coup, and to add Iraq to the U.A.R. He failed, and has
made trouble for Premier el-Kassem of Iraq ever since.

Unity, therefore, is difficult of achievement for Arabs. Indeed, abou⁺
the only issue on which they are truly united is hatred of Israel. It is
too bad that such a discordant element had to be injected into the
Middle Eastern situation.

Israel's establishment, however, was inevitable. The Western powers
had promised a Palestine territory to Zionist Jews for more than a
generation. Finally, in 1947, the United Nations voted to partition
Palestine as the best solution for Arab-Jewish tensions. The Arabs
resisted and the Zionists, fearing they would yet be denied, seized the
opportunity provided by the outbreak of fighting to set up the State

of Israel as a homeland for themselves and other displaced Jews.

This nation has come to develop against great odds, a country of the Middle East and a member of the United Nations. Her position is precarious, what with Arab pressure. So far she has survived and flourished largely by reason of financial aid received from Jews everywhere, and a flood of immigration from countries where Jews have been persecuted—notably Communist countries at the present time. But the Israeli have also demonstrated that an industrious people can prosper in a region where backward people have starved.

The Arab countries generally might profit from Israel's example. There is no reason why Arabs cannot be as productive as Jews—they stem, after all, from the same Semitic stock. The advanced agricultural and industrial methods of Israel could be employed by Arabs— and the Israeli would be more than delighted to share them. Israel's scientists and doctors are available to her neighbors, if they are wanted. Indeed, all Israel desires is the hand of friendship extended, with the promise of cooperation and peace.

But the Arab countries persist in suspicion and envy of Israel, refusing to recognize that their Israeli cousins are, actually, demonstrating what they might do for themselves.

I have had two rather interesting contacts with officials of Arabic countries, indicative of the profound misunderstanding of Israel prevalent in high places.

Sailing to Europe aboard the *S.S. Constitution* in 1958, Mr. T. J. Haycock and I fell into conversation with His Excellency Sheik Youssef Yassen, the Foreign Minister of Saudi-Arabia. Mr. Haycock, our delegate to the International Atomic Energy Agency in Geneva, kept the exchange on a diplomatic basis, but both of us felt Sheik Youssef needed correcting.

The United States, Yassen said, could no longer be friends with Saudi-Arabia because of our position and attitude towards Israel. He accused a group of four million Zionists of directing all thinking in this country, through control of radio, TV and news media. We could have prevented the 1956 attack on Egypt by Israel, Britain and France, he contended—we knew about it before it took place but did not want to stop it. Nasser was right—there would be trouble in the Middle East until Israel, as a state, had vanished. All Arab peoples feared Israeli aggression. The Jewish refugees in Israel should be sent back to their respective homelands, including East Germany. The Arabs displaced by Israel must be returned.

Mr. Haycock and I did our best to convince the Sheik he was mistaken—particularly regarding the Communist propaganda charge that the U.S. is run by a minority Zionist group, this reminiscent of similar falsehoods circulated by Hitler. As for his other anti-American accusations, I explained to him that our country does not countenance expediency in dealing with any friendly nation, and that we would no more sacrifice Israel as an expedient than we would Saudi-Arabia. How well our points got over I do not know. I don't think we succeeded in shifting the Sheik from the common Arab belief that the clock can be turned back in the Middle East, and Israel be eliminated—a sheer impossibility unless a disastrous war is to be fought.

More recently I met an intelligent young man, a Mr. el-Farra, counsellor for the Foreign Ministry of Jordan in the United Nations. He did not assail Israel but he violently attacked Zionism as a danger to the Arab world and to the Jewish religion itself. I had to agree with him that world movements like Zionism do tend to isolate their followers and disrupt peace and harmony in some national environments. But I also had to refute his contention that Zionism and Judaism are synonymous. This simply isn't true.

To describe the beauties of Israel would be pleasant, a land of plenty developed in a short period of thirteen years from a barren waste to a garden of Eden. Only those who visit there can appreciate the accomplishments.

The State of Israel was the only land where millions of displaced people were accepted without quotas and restrictions. It deserves the support of the entire world in the name of compassion and humanism. The Zionists, a section of American Judaism were the first ones to recognize the need and are responsible for much that has been done to establish this land as a homeland.

There are roaming tribes, separate and distinct from people of the European sectors who live in the backward surrounding and who wish to remain in their separate and distinct worlds. There are thousands of Arabs, Moslems and Christians who remained in Israel when hordes of their countrymen fled to the Gaza strip with the promise of their leaders that they would return when the Israel armies were beaten, that this beautiful land would be theirs and the women their slaves. Their plight is history but there are now over two hundred thousand Arabs who did not flee and are living in peace and harmony with these people, their rights and opportunities respected.

I have seen thousands of Christians and Moslems permitted to cross the border on Christmas day to worship in old Jerusalem and under the border protection of the Israel guard.

This land of Israel must not be sacrificed for selfish interests nor to buy friendships with human suffering. Israel today is a symbol of courage and determination, unsurpassed in world history. Nothing can destroy their will to live and with the memory of the crimes of the Nazi murderers, they will fight to the last man and woman to protect their land and homes. Only waste lands and destruction would remain to be conquered. Let the Arab leaders be careful that their cause of nationalism does not become a cause for bigotism.

The U.S. is very much in the middle of the Middle East. We acted as a "policeman" both in the 1956 Suez crisis and in the more recent Lebanon episode, when peace in that country was threatened. Now we seem to be stuck with the role.

No one can tell where the next difficulty may occur. Iraq has lately been the bone of contention in the fierce under-the-surface struggle between Communism and Arab nationalism—if Iraq should turn Communist, everything would be up for grabs. However, Arabs in general are alert to the fact that the Reds are not apt to aid them unselfishly.

If war should some day break out in the Middle East, we may be thankful for Israel, as a staunch friend of freedom. But we must never lose sight of an equally important item—Arab aspirations are entirely legitimate, in their end purposes, and our interests will best be served by helping them achieve those aspirations, realistically and without hatred.

Americans, with their weakness in geography, sometimes forget Egypt is an African country. So are other Arab nations, the Sudan, Libya, Tunisia, Algeria, Morocco. These are in North Africa. Africa in general is full of problems, differing from those of the Middle East and Asia only in detail. You might say that this vast continent, inhabited by many diverse peoples, all in a ferment to accomplish in a generation results it has taken the West centuries to win, is one huge sore spot from Cairo to Capetown, from Morocco to Mozambique.

Why should we concern ourselves with Africa's future? Because, if International Communism can take over here, we will be in as much trouble—or more, for the long run—than if the Reds win in Asia. The people of Africa have a much greater potential for violence, as is evidenced by the recent outbreaks in the Belgian Congo, not to mention the Mau Mau terror of not so long ago in Kenya.

The Reds are doing their utmost to make trouble, fomenting discord between blacks and whites, agitating in cities, trying to infiltrate labor unions, recruiting natives who have promise as leaders and shipping them to Communist countries for training. If Khrushchev really desires peace, let him halt Communist agitation in Africa—and in the rest of the world, for that matter—and prove his good intent.

President de Gaulle of France made a great and statesmanlike move when, in 1958, he offered the French colonies south of the Sahara a choice of going it alone or continuing to develop under French protection and guidance. Abruptly faced with the prospect of independence, for which they knew they were not ready, all but one of these primitive peoples chose to remain in the commonwealth. Guinea, more advanced than most and ambitious to head up a union of African republics, broke away. How attainable this dream of union may be is a matter of risky conjecture. Already in Ghana, until 1957 a British protectorate, Prime Minister Nkrumah has all but stamped out the democracy handed over to him and instituted a type of Marxist dictation.

De Gaulle deserves our support in his effort to keep Algeria a part of France. A war for "independence" has been waged there for more than five years—despite the wish of most Algerians as well as the French *colons* to remain French. This country has been merged with France economically for three generations; only chaos and ruin can result from separation. But again, de Gaulle and the French have offered a choice, several choices, in fact—of union with France, of a federal relationship or, after a period of peace, independence and secession. Now it is up to the Algerian rebel leaders to be statesmen.

We do not have space for a detailed discussion of African problems, nor is it necessary. With our free press, any American may read the news coming out of Africa, and judge for himself whether things are going well or ill for us there. But one critical situation does need to be mentioned—that which obtains in the Union of South Africa.

White people have been settled in South Africa since the 1600's. There has always been racial trouble; in the early times, wars with the natives, and in the nineteenth century the conquest of the northeast portions by the Boers. The whites were always outnumbered, and are still, by a black majority of nearly four to one. Deeply fearing what may happen if the aspirations of the awakening majority ever are realized, the white minority is enforcing rigid rules for the segregation of, and political and social discrimination against, all people of color.

It will never work. Already the crime rate among the coloreds is getting out of hand, and white Communists—alert as always to opportunity — seem to have convinced the political organizations of the

Negroes and the East Indian minority that only the Soviet bloc is interested in their fate. It may be that the government can keep the lid clamped on for another decade. But with the movement for African independence gathering force all through the rest of the continent, an explosion is bound to come. Unless some solution for the problem is found meanwhile—God help South Africa.

What can we do? We are struggling to ease racial barriers in our own country — and succeeding fairly well, despite the propaganda charges Communists make to the contrary. But we are in a poor position to advocate interference in South African internal affairs. Britain could far better foster corrective measures, by instigating an airing of the whole matter in the United Nations, if the reactionary government there proves unresponsive. The Union of South Africa is a nation of the British commonwealth.

The British might well feel any such suggestion on our part to be presumptuous, however. Our European allies are inclined to resent any interest we manifest in Africa.

But watch that troubled continent. The Communist world is making solid offers of aid and trade to its needy independent countries. Soon it may be too late to compete.

It is a relief to come to an area—Western Europe—where substantial progress has been made and conditions are not quite so critical. Communism has lost the battle here.

Italy's Reds, once the strongest in Europe, are steadily losing adherents to this country's conservatives. France, under de Gaulle, has a prosperity that is acquiring sound foundations with the fiscal reforms of his administration. Even Europe's socialists are in retreat, confounded by the fact of phenomenal economic recovery, no longer dependent on American aid. Britain's radicals were left without an issue in the last elections. The West German socialists have quietly buried Marxism, their standby for a hundred years, since the contrast between East Germany's poverty and West Germany's boom has demonstrated its inherent fallacies.

West Germany is not entirely secure. The recent outbreak of anti-Semitism there is symptomatic. Visitors have reported that many of the people still regret Hitler's failure, still feel themselves a superior race. The present liberal government has moved energetically to stamp out these renascent evidences of Nazism, and probably with some reason, attributed them to Communist agitation. The Communists would do anything to discredit the Adenauer regime. But it is evi-

dently also true that a reservoir of hate is left in Germany. The people
need to learn, once and for all, that hate leads to self-destruction, that
the Hitlerian crime in which they joined was directed as much against
themselves as against the world.

However, the rest of the world is not guiltless, either. It is very
disturbing to note how quickly German attacks on Jews and desecra-
tion of synagogues were echoed elsewhere, even in Iowa. Were these
incidents Communist-inspired? Hate would seem to be a universal
poison, and a lunatic minority always present to raise their heads in
ugliness.

There will be unrest in both Germanies as long as the nation remains
divided. And a divided Germany is symbolic of divided Europe, with
half of a region which in the interests of peace should be united, cut
off by the Iron Curtain. Despite the economic health of Western
Europe, Europe as a whole will continue sick until the Iron Curtain
countries can be freed, and reoriented to the West where lies their
heritage.

In Berlin this reality is demonstrated daily. West Berlin is an
economic salient, a showcase for the superiority of the Western way of
life. East Berlin is a prison where Germans must live in rigidly
policed squalor, poorly clothed, underpaid for work norms set by the
Russian puppets, constantly fearing that infractions of the rules may
cost them their food cards. If they try to escape, their families suffer
for their daring. Such a state of affairs cannot exist indefinitely, in
Berlin, in Germany, or in Europe.

Many highly skilled East German workers, Party defectors and
others necessary to the Red regime, have fled through this gateway
to the West. It is a hole in the Iron Curtain for intelligence that
Russia doesn't want to leak. But most of all, the Berlin situation is
intolerable to Khrushchev because it furnishes continual evidence of
the failures of Communism.

What will happen is difficult to foresee. Khrushchev used the threat
of forcing the West out of the city to bludgeon his way to his U.S.
visit—and to maneuver us into agreeing to the summit meetings he
has so long desired. Now the pressure has eased somewhat. But you
may depend on it that he will not be content until Berlin is closed off.

From our viewpoint, retention of our foothold there is vital. If we
give up West Berlin, it will be a death blow not only to Allied prestige
but to the hopes of all Iron Curtain prisoners. The threat of force
will have won.

But the Berlin issue can make a good ground for negotiation towards the free unification of Germany, and perhaps a united Germany would make a good place to begin on the program of disarmament Khrushchev loudly proclaims is his objective, in addition to his wish for "peaceful co-existence."

Consider what this might mean for Russia and for the German people, not to mention the peoples of the Russian satellites when once the principle of disarmament is logically extended.

Let us make no bones about it: Russia is justified in fearing the might of a rearmed Germany. Adenauer cannot live forever, and if another Hitler should arise it could mean the beginning of World War III. But a Germany freely united, prosperous and unarmed—protected only by the might of the West—would surely be loath to become a battleground again.

In return for an unthreatening Germany, the Soviets would have to follow suit and demilitarize the Iron Curtain countries, thereby creating a vast belt—Central Europe, the hotbed of most past wars—free of armaments. If Khrushchev is sincere in his demand for disarming, he could surely have no objection to this arrangement for beginning the effort, together with adequate inspection and guarantees.

The Russians have boggled at inspection of their own military installations in disarmament talks. Very well, let us all try it out in a Germany united, and in the satellites.

Then let us negotiate for world-wide disarmament and abolition of the atomic weapons that keep the peoples of the world in continual trepidation.

In the beginning arrangements suggested in the foregoing, France would have to play a central part. France is the keystone of Western Europe, geographically, politically and industrially. A mere look at the map shows that without France, the North Atlantic Treaty Organization cannot exist.

We have problems in this hemisphere. Argentina needs more help in struggling out of the wreckage left by Peron. Our trade with Brazil is vital to us, and Brazil has the strongest Communist Party in South America. Latin American populations are expected to quadruple in the next fifty years. Would it not be well to have seven hundred and fifty million Latin American friends in 2010?

A great deal of the shape of the future will depend on how we handle the Cuban situation. Friendship for Cuba's people must be evident in anything we do. Other peoples of this hemisphere regard themselves as Americans too. They call us North Americans. They, like ourselves, are inheritors of the freedom that came to the hemisphere in throwing off the yoke of the old world.

In the past, many of us have felt a certain scorn for Latin Americans because of their political instability. However, we have been luckier than they, not only in our sound political heritage but in climate and resources. Now most of our southern neighbors have achieved governmental responsibility and what they need is accelerated commercial development plus a more acute understanding that "freedom is their business" in these days when it is so sorely threatened.

U.S. policy towards our hemisphere is probably more vital than our relations with the rest of the world. Apart from any world policy, a comprehensive program for the extension of aid and the economic improvement of Latin America should be launched as the most effective means of combatting Red subversion. At the same time we should firmly let it be known that we cannot and will not tolerate power vacuums exploitable by International Communism.

What we may need is an extension of the Monroe Doctrine suited to the changing conditions of modern times. The world has known for more than a century that we will resist by force of arms any attempt of a foreign power to seize territory in the Western hemisphere. Similarly, it is now appropriate for us to state than any wild-eyed terror at our doorstep is tantamount to an invasion of our shores.

As President Eisenhower has said, "Peace and friendship, in freedom" is our national aim. This does not mean hemispheric peace at any cost, nor the acceptance of abuse by Communist-dominated dictators such as Castro. We can only gain further contempt by taking it.

Fateful issues hang on our relations with Latin America. If our hemisphere does not remain free eventually there will be no freedom.

In substance, we must make it clear that no violation of our Monroe Doctrine will be tolerated, that invasion or infiltration by Communist forces will be met with force. When England was the world power no one ever wronged an Englishman without retaliation. We must stop seeking world favor and demand world respect. We must care what the rest of the world thinks of us, providing that we survive.

IX

OUR SYSTEM HAS SORE SPOTS, TOO

A freedom seldom mentioned by anybody—but one that exerts influence on quite a few others—is freedom from overwhelming debt. Reasonable indebtedness is one thing, no one can boggle at it. But America's prosperity since World War II, unprecedented even when we allow for two minor recessions, has led our people into a wrongheaded attitude of complacency toward our total national bill. We have no reason to be complacent. Government obligations have very nearly reached disastrous proportions. In really bad times, they could ruin us.

Let me cite a few figures. As of September, 1959, the national debt hit the astronomical level of $290 billion—$1,641.52 for every man, woman and child in the U.S. Interest charges alone top nine billion dollars annually, an average cost of $275 to every taxpaying American family. Congressional studies indicate that it will require at least one hundred and fifty years to pay off the total under present conditions, which is a disgraceful legacy to leave our children. Of course, this period could be shortened radically if the cold war came to an end, if there were no more wars or depressions, and if we made a determined effort to economize. The trend of government in the last generation, however, has been toward more and more extravagances.

Some economic theorists contend that we owe this money to ourselves, and so needn't worry about it. Do they mean to imply we can forget the interest charges, too? At the current rate we will have paid out $290 billion in little more than thirty years just for the privilege of owing it. They're wrong in their basic premise, anyway. This money is owed by us as a nation to individuals and financial institutions in our society, and if our national credit is no good we as a nation will sooner or later go down the drain.

A look at the tax structure in this country is illuminating. All of us are making more money these days, but we are also paying more of it to the government. Twenty-five years ago 21% of our national income went for taxes; today the tax bill amounts to 31% of everything we receive. The federal government takes three-fourths of all taxes today as opposed to one-fourth twenty-five years ago, which shows how extreme is our drift toward centralization. But the really weird thing about our tax structure is the cost of its "soak the rich" philosophy, and 27% of our people pay income tax, two out of three of these in the lowest bracket. Did you know that a very small minority of citizens pay a confiscatory rate of 91% on taxable income over $200,000? Now, you may feel that anyone who makes more than $200,000 a year ought to have it taken away from him. But did you know also that all income tax revenue above the basic 20% rate yields the Treasury only $5,000,000,000 out of a total $40,000,000,000? And that if the confiscatory rates in the top brackets were reduced to 60% the Treasury would actually get more money?

This may sound odd, but the answer is simple. Our "soak the rich" philosophy is robbing the country of risk capital. It takes about $14,000 in new capital to create a single job in industry. Thousands of jobs—nearly seventy thousand, in fact—could be created in this country if only a billion dollars of risk capital could be left in the economy each year. The holders of these jobs would pay taxes, the new corporations employing them would pay taxes, the capitalists owning the corporations would pay taxes, and so on. It really builds.

Many commercial ventures have been abandoned before they even got started in this country because people with money cannot balance out risk against return, the tax situation being what it is. Would you want to invest money that might be lost, for a net profit of less than 1%? That is what some of our capitalists are being asked to do. Naturally, they refuse. They can do better by staying with established enterprises.

And so the new ventures don't happen, the new jobs are not created, the new taxes are not forthcoming. While, at the same time, we have more and more people growing up who need those new jobs in order to enjoy full living.

Another iniquitous facet of our tax structure is that it robs imaginative and productive people of incentive. Often talented individuals have risked much to accept promotions—changed jobs, moved their families, taken on new headaches—and found that half or more of their increase in pay must be given up to the government. Undoubtedly many more such people have refused advances because they couldn't be made worthwhile from an income standpoint. Why should a man be penalized for widening his field of service?

And, entirely too often, important business decisions hinge on the tax angle, so that less productive expedients are adopted as a matter of sheer survival. I would be the last to suggest that corporations and their more highly paid employees should not be taxed. But let our tax structure be revised so that our economy can operate freely in the interests of all.

Actually, the people carry the largest share of the tax burden. Only one American out of 100 has a taxable income of over $15,000. The average man pays about $5 in taxes from every day's pay—and inflation has more than wiped out any pay increases he's had in the last ten or so years. That's the final iniquity—our tax system is inflationary.

I've had things to say about inflation in other portions of this book, but those references were mostly to runaway inflation, the kind that impoverishes people so desperately that they overthrow their government. Ours has been called a "creeping" inflation, and some theorists feel we can tolerate it. I don't—not when the purchasing power of the dollar has declined by about one-half in the last twenty-five years.

Historically, inflation has long been with us. Wars are always inflationary. Goods become scarce, prices rise, and when the fighting is over money is never worth what it was before unless vigorous efforts are made to restore its value. We haven't made the effort. Inflation has been too convenient a way of paying, in part, for every war we've had—including the Revolution. Patriotic lenders to our government, and purchasers of bonds, have invariably been paid off in depreciated dollars, and thus have contributed a disproportionate share of war costs.

Inflation has robbed World War II bond buyers not only of interest to which they had a right but of part of the value of the very dollars they "invested" during the conflict. It takes two dollars now to buy what one bought in 1940. Inflation does other damaging things to us. It places a heavy burden on government in financing loans. Once started, an inflationary trend is difficult to stop, and government securities are simply not a good investment. Right now, the little people who ordinarily buy Series E and H savings bonds are backing away from them; there are 42 billion dollars of these outstanding, and if the holders began to cash them in the Treasury would be in straits. As for long-term Treasury bonds, not a single issue is selling at par these days; some have been quoted as low as 81, which means that they have already incurred a loss of 19%, if purchased at par. In the current fiscal year our government is borrowing huge sums on short term securities at higher interest rates. The additional cost comes out of the taxpayer—you.

Inflation boosts interest rates on all loans, especially mortgages. If

you've tried to negotiate a real estate loan recently, you've probably
been asked to pay interest of 7% or 8%. Nowadays, sellers of homes
with FHA or GI mortgages as a rule have to pay out from 1% to 4%
or more of the market value of their property to transfer their loan to
a purchaser. This is one way of protecting the lender against inflation
because he is taking the risk that the dollars he is paid won't be worth
the dollars he has lent.

Inflation hurts us internationally—not only does it bring about a
loss of confidence in the dollar abroad, but if it continues we will inevitably price ourselves out of world markets, asking more and more
dollars for less and less value. In an inflationary bind, manufacturers
tend to cheapen goods.

Inflation retards our national growth, in that it destroys the value of
savings as well as discouraging savers. In this country savings have
always been the principal source of capital for long-term investment—
housing, schools, utilities, roads and so forth. Today there are 180
million Americans, by 1975 or so we may number well over 225 million—say 45-50 million more people needing stores, hospitals, public
transportation, things to be financed out of savings. Where will the
savings come from if inflation isn't halted?

Inflation brings misery to older citizens with fixed incomes. It
destroys the value of insurance policies. It can make your Social
Security payments next to worthless, by the time you begin drawing
them. It is of vital concern to every American, and the "creeping"
kind is the most insidious.

Believe me, we can "creep" our way into bankruptcy.

It is entirely possible to curb inflation. In France, prices soared
for forty years while the franc depreciated until, last year, it was
worth about two-thousandths of a cent. Yet former foreign minister
Antoine Pinay and his successor, Wilfrid Baumgartner of the Bank
of France, have reversed the process.

With de Gaulle's backing, Pinay slashed expenditures, balanced the
national budget, invented a new "heavy" franc he pegged to gold
rather than the dollar, and began overhauling the tax system to eliminate loopholes and inequities. We need to do the same things, including putting our dollar back on the gold standard.

More importantly, Pinay undertook a couple of basic reforms,
attacking inflation where it begins.

First, he went to work getting rid of most of the government subsidies that for years had been recklessly paid out to industry and agri-

culture. We haven't gone in so much for industrial handouts, but our farm supports need correcting.

This business, the most reckless extravagance in which Americans have ever indulged, has cost us $18 billion in twenty-five years. Right now, out of every tax dollar over and above defense spending, twenty cents goes to farm supports. Nine billion dollars of public funds is invested in surpluses. It costs us a billion dollars a year for storage and related expenses. Another $5.4 billion was laid out for agriculture in 1959, with the bulk of it going to factories-in-the-field that shouldn't need subsidizing. It has come to light lately that a substantial portion of the land held out of production in our "soil bank" should never have been included in that part of the farm program. Payments are being made on some acreage that hasn't been cultivated for years, anyway, or is submarginal and unfit for use.

A popular impression is that many inefficient farmers are being kept on submarginal land by subsidies. This isn't nearly as true as you might think. According to an editorial in *Life* for January 11, 1960: "Only 600,000 farms turn out nearly three-fifths of all marketed farm products (dollar value); only two million produce 90% and could easily turn out all of it. . . . The two-million-odd other farmers who turn out less than 10% of our marketed crops are too poor or unproductive even to qualify for subsidies." Most of them obviously should be in some other line of work.

It may be, as some argue, that we have put our agriculture so far out of kilter with subsidies that our economy would collapse if we halted the program abruptly. However, could we not make a start somewhere? Most productive farmers themselves are disgusted with the support mess. It isn't helping them. While the government pours out the dollars and surpluses accumulate, their net income is declining.

With prices and wages constantly leap-frogging each other, what can we achieve but inflation? This is not to say that the larger responsibility for our creeping inflation should be laid at the door of American labor, by any means. America as a whole is responsible.

Inflation would not have come upon us at all without the consent of an ill-informed, apathetic electorate. Government, management and labor have contributed but in the final analysis the people are the government, the people are management, and the people are labor. The blame must be shared by all of us.

Until recently the people of this country demanded a deliberately inflationary government policy. A good many still do. After the war everyone wanted things they had been denied during it; they wanted to buy things they really couldn't afford. They insisted on easy money and bank credits were permitted to get out of hand. The Federal Reserve system has now had to clamp down on credits and increase interest rates, which is the only way to restrain over-spending, which, if unrestrained, has the effect of printing money and devaluing our currency. Meanwhile much damage has been done.

Government is still being subjected to demands for expenditures exceeding income and Congress has been lax in not providing taxes to equal expenditures. The outlook for fiscal 1961 is good. President Eisenhower even hopes for a budgetary surplus of more than $4 billion with which to begin reducing the national debt. But will Congress abstain from spending it? It should be obvious that, as a nation, we cannot continue living beyond our means, and that the time has come to conserve our resources and, in a year of prosperity, to pay instead of spend. Otherwise inflation will keep spiraling upward. Only the people can call a halt to it.

The people *can* obtain Congressional respect for their wishes between elections, you know. They did it about a year ago, when the anti-racketeering labor law was about to be side-tracked. Congress got so much mail in favor of it that fairly effective legislation was passed in a hurry. And the promise of public support caused management, finally, to take a stand against inflation in the subsequent steel strike.

Discussion of a few basics regarding government, management and labor is appropriate at this point.

Since the turn of the century, labor has made great progress in organization and the gaining of economic strength. The labor movement has brought many benefits to workers, and to the American people. More or less concurrently with labor's rise, the unbridled power of business was curbed, and this too has been an excellent, constructive thing. Then, in the 1930's, a swing of the political pendulum resulted in enactment of legislation which further restrained business and, in effect, granted labor the power, through its unions, to enforce whatever demands union leaders felt they might safely make.

This legislation, ostensibly designed to promote industrial peace, did not accomplish its purpose—there were three times as many strikes after its passage. And it placed government in the role of referee between union leaders and business management. A pattern was established by which government was hard put to hold an anti-inflationary line. Indeed, public pressure often caused an administration to encourage management to raise wages beyond the level of productivity, and to pass costs along to the public in higher places.

Other inflationary forces, such as farm subsidies—and notably those engendered by World War II — have accelerated the upward spiral. But somehow the spurts have always seemed to stem from rounds of wage increases, throughout industry, set off by the settlement of steel strikes in favor of labor.

Not that the finger of shame should be pointed at the steel industry, necessarily. It is simply that steel is our most basic commodity, and price increases in steel are reflected all along the line.

In labor disputes of the last fifteen years, management hasn't measured up to its responsibilities generally. Yet it is difficult to blame corporate leaders for yielding to union demands when they have had neither governmental nor public support. Besides, their personal fortunes have seldom been involved, as their chief rewards usually come from stock holdings which are hardly affected by inflation. Many of them have been worried by the trends in our economy, and have warned the people that trouble lay ahead. But few Americans heeded them. Not until last year did business begin to exercise the conservative leadership it should—when definite signs of public concern over what has been happening became evident.

Union leaders have not shown any great sense of responsibility, either. But this, too, is understandable. Conditioned to winning strikes, as a rule, they have come to feel it is their right to win, and any opposing them must therefore be wrong. They are under considerable pressure, also, to demand more and more benefits. Most union leaders rise from the ranks of labor, fighting their way up through the rough-and-tumble of recruiting and organizing, and if they fail to get results in negotiations, other leaders eager for power are always pushing from beneath.

And labor champions generally are somewhat socialistic. They believe the cause of labor sacred, and regard management as the enemy, the exploiter. A constant cry among them is that higher wages can and should be paid out of profits.

Is this contention true? A statement by the National Association of Manufacturers—and surely management has a right to speak in the matter—is illuminating.

First, the federal government takes more than half of all profits. Many states also take a share; sometimes a single company is taxed on profits by many states. About half of what remains is plowed back into the companies. Some of it goes into research, more into plant replacement and expansion—preparation for growth tomorrow. What is left goes for dividends, the rightful reward of millions of Americans who have invested their savings, of insurance companies who own stock, of universities, and even of labor union welfare funds. Dividends must be paid or capital, the lifeblood of industry, will be cut off.

And here are a couple of interesting facts. In 1959, in steel, the workers' increased pay outstripped dividend increase by 86 to 1. Again, in steel, since World War II wages have increased an average of 6% to 8% yearly, while productivity by each worker, on the average, has gone up only 2%.

Since 1945 steel workers have lost more in actual income, as a result of strikes, than they've gained in wage increases. It is estimated that up until last year their idle time cost them more than $830 million, very little of which was recovered in strike gains. In the lengthy 1959 strike they lost about $1 billion in wages—and besides, nearly $3 billion was lost in steel sales, lost production amounted to 27½ million tons, and $630 million was lost in taxes.

It would appear that such strikes are an extravagance this nation can no longer afford. Everybody loses—the strikers themselves, industry, the economy, and all Americans plus those yet to be born.

Faced with these facts, our labor leaders are in a dilemma. Some of them have become angry, accusing business of a 'conspiracy' to destroy labor, threatening dire things in the way of more and rougher strikes. I do not believe they are out to wreck us, as some equally angry spokesmen for industry have claimed. But they can end by wrecking their unions, forcing permanent government intervention in labor relations, and losing freedoms of utmost value to this country.

Is the answer to be further legislation, curbing union power? This may be necessary. Conrad Cooper of U.S. Steel had a point when he said that no man in the management of any steel company could shut down the American steel industry—not even the President of the United States could do that—but one man could, and that man was the president of the steel workers' union.

However, there's another answer, one that involves a basic change in attitude—and this must come with or without legislation. Labor and management must come to realize that they are not enemies but partners. Business is just a part of our American system, not a separate entity. No more is labor a separate entity. With doctors and teachers and shopkeepers and farmers, business and labor make up a team contributing to the general welfare, including their own.

Labor leaders have helped the individual to earn more. Business leaders have helped the individual to buy more. Big business is necessary for the production of heavy machinery, research and manufacturing where large capital is required. Big unions are necessary to negotiate with big business, to even up the score. But "big" also means "great", and greatness should carry a connotation of mental and moral endowments that have not been too evident in the relations of management and labor up to this date.

The public has a vital stake in labor-management relations, and that means, people, you and I, everybody. Let labor and management realize that they have an obligation to people. For that matter, why shouldn't representatives of the public sit in on labor-management negotiations and have a voice in the decisions made? Strangely enough, I have a feeling that management would welcome this proposal more than would our labor leaders, who are presumably devoted to the welfare of people.

Far too many union bosses still hold to the Marxist premise that business exploits labor. The exploitation of labor by management is not true today. In my experience as a businessman it has never been true. American labor receives by far the largest share of the rewards of our production. In constantly demanding more, labor is beginning to emulate the fabled lad who killed the goose that laid the golden eggs.

Perhaps labor needs to recognize that people in management are also workers. Indeed, few executives of my experience have ever been able to limit themselves to an eight-hour day or a five-day week.

It might not be harmful, occasionally, to give a second thought to the industrious men of management, the job-creators in our system, of whom it may truly be said that "labor is their business".

The tragedy of the disastrous steel strike of 1959 is that it was not concerned so much with wage increases or fringe benefits, but with the issue of make-work practices, or "featherbedding". This peculiar term came into use many years ago when a freight train crew on a midwestern railroad complained to their conductor about the cornshuck filled mattresses then common. He snapped, "What do you want—feather beds?" and the expression stuck.

Incidentally, did you ever try to sleep on a cornshuck mattress? As the shucks dry out, they stab one. Those trainmen merely wanted ordinary cotton pads.

The railroad industry was one of the earliest to take up automation, the process by which mechanical devices replace hand labor. The rail unions were strong enough to resist the displacement of workers who should have moved on to other jobs, in or out of railroading. There was room for them in our expanding economy, and there still is. Railroad management, helpless against union power, could only retaliate by labeling the retention of unnecessary labor as "featherbedding".

The industry is beset by make-work to this day. Idle firemen twiddle their thumbs on Diesel locomotives, and crews are changed needlessly on today's speedier trains. Work rules boost costs in switch yards when one may do only this, another only that. Featherbedding on railroads costs about $500 millions a year, roughly 10% of the total payroll, while this nation's heavy carriers are trying to survive as a utility indispensable in war and vital to our economy at any time. Most of our freight moves on rails.

In the past decade or so, automation has made rapid progress in industry of all kinds—as the term "featherbedding" has spread wherever make-work rules persist. Unions hate it, and with good reason for it implies dishonesty.

Featherbedding *is* dishonest. It amounts to getting paid for work that isn't done and insisting on that pay. It is morally wrong, a sort of pistol at the head of industry. Are the unions entirely at fault?

Labor fears automation. The displacement of workers by automatic processes is a threat to union power. So far in actual experience, automation has increased employment as well as production; but in an extreme example it might be that large numbers of workers would lose their jobs through the rapid conversion of a factory, and union membership be thus dispersed. This hasn't happened yet to my knowledge.

But labor does have a legitimate complaint in that business has not concerned itself particularly with the problem of displaced workers—that is, finding them equal or better jobs, whether in a particular industry or elsewhere. It has been easier for management to go along with featherbedding, once more yielding to union demands, in most cases. The waste? Another cost to be passed along to the public.

We can't afford that waste any more, with its contribution to spiraling inflation. We can't afford waste at all, in our present posture of competition with foreign industry.

There is a general belief that foreign products are less expensive than ours mainly because of lower labor costs abroad. This is an oversimplification. While in Japan I was asked by an American manufacturer of heavy machinery how the Japanese could underbid him in world markets by some 30% when the labor cost of that product was only 10%. The answer became evident when we looked for it: the Japanese had the advantages of higher production per man, lower overhead, lower taxes and greater sales volume.

The same advantages are possessed in varying degrees by England, West Germany, France and other countries. So America is faced today with a serious flight of capital abroad, with many of our large companies opening foreign plants so as to compete successfully in those markets. Our exports are correspondingly reduced, and if the situation is aggravated or even continues at the present level our entire economy can come to grief.

Protective tariffs will do us no good. They merely isolate us commercially and provoke retaliation, so that our exports have a still more difficult time abroad. We can only put ourselves in a better competitive position here at home. This means tax reform and stern government economy. More importantly, perhaps, it demands increased productivity all along the line—which means just plain hard work—and putting an end to inflationary wage scales and such egregious wastes as featherbedding.

This may not be so peculiar a term, after all. I don't expect everyone to agree, but it seems to me that Americans are a little too fond of their featherbeds. The urge to get something for nothing causes constant pressure on Congress for more unearned benefits— apparently in the fatuous belief that the money will come out of the other fellow's pocket. The craze for quiz shows on television was indicative of the great American yearning for windfalls. We have even encouraged our children to play their way through school, educating them 'progressively'—which means, so far as I find out, that the less progressive are protected in the name of equality, with easy courses given preference over the vital hard ones. Other instances of 'featherbedding' in our culture could be cited, but all you have to do is look around you—you'll find them.

What is needed? Well, we can take a searching look at ourselves and begin to correct our deficiencies as a people.

But more than that, what is needed is a recognition of individual responsibility, the responsibility we all of us bear, if a strong and free America is to continue as a leader in the world community.

X

RESPONSIBILITIES OF THE INDIVIDUAL

It has often occurred to me that we could possibly copy some Communist tactics with success in the present situation. I mean the use of shock treatment—hot one day and cold the next. Our course seems to be conciliatory one day and temperate the next. Communists consider this a weakness—though it must be admitted this impression is encouraged by the utterances of some politicans. It would improve our foreign relations greatly if the world were made to understand once and for all that official American policy may be recognized only in our official statements.

The key to improved international understanding of America would seem to lie in improved communications. Our past and present efforts in that direction have not been too successful. One of our lacks is that we have not found many positive themes for our propaganda, or that we have not employed them well.

Closed socities are an anomaly today. We live in a world in which the transmission of information is instantaneous. It is impossible for a people to live in isolation, without knowledge of other peoples, nor can the truth about any people, or system, or regime, long remain unknown. Nor should it; with the dire possibilities for world destruction coming within reach of so many hands, all too soon, accurate information about all the peoples of the world will become imperative for the survival of mankind. This applies with special force to Communist nations.

The Communists are especially dedicated to the "closed society" concept, for the simple reason that they must control the thinking of their peoples about their system if it is to endure. There are too many contradictions between preachment and practice in that system, not to mention the differences between facts in the outside world and Red interpretation of them, for any thinking person to swallow. Thus, in Communist countries, information cannot be permitted to flow freely, or the topsy-turvy Marxist world will be exposed for what it is—an arrangement for unrestrained exploitation of the many in the interests of the few.

It is my belief that in the long run we would even destroy the Communists—or expedite their self-destruction by using incessant and accurate exposure as our principal weapon. This might be done, of course, only from a position of strength. Long before we approached success with our strategy of destruction-by-exposure with Communist populations disillusioned and rebellious, the leaders frustrated in gaining adherents by their wholesale lies and their denigration of the West, Russia and China would, I am sure, attempt to levy atomic blackmail on the rest of the world in a bid for supremacy. If, that is, they thought they could get away with it. And so we cannot renounce our capability of destroying their half of the world by force either, unless there is actually hope of effective disarmament—a dim prospect.

However, I doubt that the enemy will ever dare an atomic holocaust. Rather, they will attempt to wear us down in the so-called "small" wars, or by cut-throat competition in the fields of trade. But no matter what happens, our propaganda effort should be aimed at continual and complete exposure.

The Communists are peculiarly vulnerable. The only security they have to offer mankind is that of slavery. And they cannot hope to maintain their "closed society" against the means of communication which characterize the world today. They may use these channels to transmit lies—but lies can be refuted via the same channels. A basic theme we can hammer on is this business of the "closed society" itself. Why is it necessary if Communist claims of superiority are true? A closed society is a secret thing, a danger to the world, a thing hidden because it is poisonous. What are they concealing behind their Iron and Bamboo Curtains? Why do they want to hide things if they don't mean harm? Why, indeed, do they object so vociferously to U-2s photographing their launching sites if they don't mean to attack the world treacherously?

All I am saying is that we must carry the propaganda battle vigorously to the enemy if we hope to win it at all. The weight of truth is on our side. We must proclaim it to the world, explaining our acts and our motives, exposing Communist falsities and the crimes they commit against freedom everywhere. If we refuse to be turned from the truth, eventually truth must and will prevail. If Russian Communism can survive with the truth, let them prove it.

What we have in our democracy is new and promising; what they have is autocracy, old and evil. They dare not open their system to free inquiry as we do every day with our free press. But we can force them to it in some degree, perhaps, by subjecting them to such merciless questioning that they must defend themselves, and reveal

themselves in that defense. At the same time we must show ourselves to other peoples as we see ourselves, and gain the understanding
and respect of this world on something approaching our own terms.
That we should constantly find ourselves in a posture of defense is
not only crippling but shameful.

And to add to our own efforts to spread the truth, a world church
movement could be one of the greatest forces as a forum to meet the
atheist philosophy of world Communism. In this move the church
cannot fail but they must make a new combined effort of such proportions that their voice can be heard around the world.

A more enlightened citizenry will be a more alert citizenry, and
a rising generation schooled in world viewpoints and the diplomatic
facts of life will furnish more and better candidates for this country's
service. In England's day of world leadership she had at her command the finest corps of representatives abroad any country ever
possessed. They were men of background and culture, men supremely
well educated and prepared for their jobs. The State Department
of this country has taken steps to improve the training of our foreign
service people. Would it not be a great advantage to have them come
already partially trained, ingrained with the knowledge and habits
of thought necessary to American survival in this most perplexing
and dangerous age?

This country has not had the advantage of possessing a distinct
class of gentlemen dedicated to public service, such as has England.
But then, the Communists cannot boast a brigade of gentlemen,
either. It is my fervent hope that we may have a foreign service
corps and information people equally as dedicated as England's,
and that never again shall we Americans find ourselves so far behind
in the propaganda contest,—maligned and misunderstood in too many
quarters of the world, and in some cases even mistrusted by our
friends.

There are other sore spots in our system. Our growing crime rate
is one, and it is especially alarming in that it reflects a breakdown
of national morality, for the incidence of crime of all sorts far out-
strips the rate of population growth. However, a situation which
seems to me more alarming is the supine, lethargic attitude so many
Americans reflect towards anything not immediately concerned with
their personal lives.

I have thought a long time about this chapter of our book, hating
the idea that I might begin to sermonize. I shall try to avoid
scolding, having found in a fairly long life that it seldom, if ever,

does any good. However, let us consider some shortcomings all of us manifest from time to time.

For instance, the matter of plain citizenship.

Our average American seems to take his freedoms pretty much for granted. He realizes dimly that his forefathers fought, bled and died so that he might enjoy these freedoms; he knows that millions of other Americans, and perhaps he himself, went off to fight two wars with the idea of saving the world for democracy—the second because the first one failed to accomplish its purpose. He knows, or he should know, that the issue still isn't settled, and that International Communism now threatens him, either with absorption or annihilation. He certainly knows that a substantial portion of his income goes to pay for American defense and foreign aid programs.

But does the average citizen know that the defense of his freedoms begins at home? That retaining his freedoms depends on what he does as a citizen?

It isn't so hard to exercise our voting privilege—a matter of fifteen minutes to stop and cast a ballot, when you know who and what you're voting for. Of course, it takes more time to bone up on political personalities and the facts. But maybe your kids can help you. They get quite a bit in school about election issues—some of it not entirely correct.

That's just the beginning, though. If our hypothetical average American is truly interested in his freedoms—and those his children will have when he is gone—he follows up on the activities and voting records of his representatives in Congress, in state legislatures, county boards, municipal councils. This may not be quite so easy, though all you have to do about your man in Congress is send him a card, and he'll usually put you on his mailing list for newsletters. Perhaps you'll have to read your paper carefully to find out about your state and local representatives—and it pays to read between the lines. Then if you don't like what you read, it pays to drop these people a line of your own.

Believe me, nothing has so salutary an effect on the elected as to realize that constituents are keeping track of them between elections.

This is too much trouble? You don't know what trouble is, friends, until you see the trouble that comes to people around this world who must get along *without* representatives.

We won't have to worry about that as long as we exercise our rights as American citizens. The world-wide trend towards big government and statism may be inevitable, even in this country—but we can all retain our share in big government, and defeat the dictatorial aspects of statism, by making our voices heard, continually and insistently.

If, on the other hand, prosperity has lulled us into insensibility to our interests as individuals, we can wake up to find our country changed in ways we don't want.

To my mind, most of the ills that have overtaken the world in our time are directly attributable to prejudice, intolerance and hate. Adolf Hitler didn't invent the technique of whipping up baser human emotions in order to incite to conquest, nor did the Communists. These weaknesses of humanity have been exploited by power-seeking demagogues since the dawn of history. But Hitler and Stalin practiced their malign arts with great success, and they left the world a legacy of hate from which even we Americans are not immune.

Hatreds engendered by World War II divide our country to this day—witness the bitterness between labor and management. Differences of opinion are natural, but when they are permitted to develop into such intractable antipathies as we have seen in the recent steel dispute, so that the very foundations of our system are threatened, it is time to call a halt.

Shall we examine something of the anatomy of prejudice, intolerance and hate? They are actually the same thing, in differing degrees of expression.

We are all guilty of harboring prejudice, to some extent. It springs from ignorance; and, after all, no man can know everything. I'm fond of saying that prejudice is being down on something you're not up on. Nevertheless, the individual invariably feels his prejudices are justified, even when they are figments of the imagination. When our prejudices happen to be challenged, we usually react unscientifically, and so prejudice easily hardens into intolerance. We say to ourselves (or to other people), "I'm right, and that fool is wrong, and if he insists on being stupid he can't expect me to do anything about it." In more extreme cases, intolerance becomes hatred, and then something very often *is* done about it, usually wrong.

It isn't easy to combat these attitudes. Most of us encounter frustration in our lives, and when we're frustrated we get resentful. Instinctively we try to find an outlet for our resentment, especially if it isn't possible to vent it against the causative prejudice or intolerance, just to get it out of our systems. The trouble is, we are almost always doing somebody else an injustice in thus blowing off steam.

When this sort of thing gets going on a community or a national scale, it's really bad. Widespread frustration is readily fanned into active hate. It starts with a whisper and ends with a shriek. Some of you may remember the speeches Hitler used to make—shrieking diatribes of hate. The German people answered him by shrieking for war.

In the final analysis, though, it all comes back to the individual. Hitler's appeal for violence was addressed to individuals. If it were not for individual response, magnified as it was communicated from person to person, his inflammatory message would have died echoless.

Isn't it tragic that hate is so much more communicable than love? It may be that humanity hasn't yet advanced to the point where the practice of universal love can find much acceptance, but as individuals we can certainly profit by the advice the great teacher Gautama Buddha imparted to his followers some twenty-five hundred years ago.

Said Buddha: "Believe nothing, O monks, merely because you have been told it, or because it is traditional or because you yourselves have imagined it. Do not believe what your teacher tells you merely out of respect for the teacher. But whatsoever, after due examination and analysis, you find to be conducive to the good, the benefit, the welfare of all beings, that doctrine believe and cling to, and take it as your guide."

That's solid, and it's practical. We can every one of us examine our prejudices, intolerances and hates in such a light—and act accordingly.

Bigotry has a way of rebounding against the bigot. Not only does he curdle himself, but every time he assails the rights of others he assails his own rights. As has been mentioned earlier, every right entails an obligation to see that that right is enjoyed also by your neighbor. Otherwise he is not apt to return the favor, considering it selfishly.

Most bigotry stems from class associations. Once people are classified by race, color or creed, they begin to lose identity as individuals. Often, in the popular mind, traits are assigned to groups, nationalities or religions which may not be particularly attractive to others. This is an error, to begin with; it is highly inaccurate. And the moment we judge an individual by so-called group traits, or classify him socially, we are robbing him of his individual dignity and worth.

If people are to be classified at all, let it be by their worth as individuals. That's the democratic way. And it's the only way of defending their dignity, and yours.

The concept of the dignity and worth of the individual is in part religious—as, indeed, American democracy is founded on the idea of 'one nation under God.' Unfortunately there exists a good deal of prejudice within some religious groups. Interfaith relationships and brotherhoods are doing much to break down such influences toward disunity among individuals (it must be said that very few ministers, priests or rabbis subscribe to them) and to promote mutual understanding and respect. Much more could be done by people who do considerable talking about 'fellowship' but seldom practice it, or, if they do practice it, care little whether others do.

Actually, the rooting out of prejudice and intolerance in America is a matter for careful and continuous education. Class distinction such as exists in the South certainly cannot be changed by legislation alone. Nor, it seems to me, should integration in Southern schools have begun largely at the high school and college levels. How much simpler it would have been to start with the earliest grades, or kindergarten, when the individual still thinks for himself and has not had time to learn prejudices. Such a program would not have fostered fanatic reactions and, continuing through successive school years, would seem to answer the Supreme Court's demand for integration 'with all deliberate speed.' In any case, Southern leaders have a problem in achieving acceptance of integration, and others in this nation might better try to understand than condemn them.

The National Association for the Advancement of Colored People might do a better job if less emphasis were placed on agitation and more on the responsibility members of the race have for self-improvement. Take the episode concerning Dr. Ralph Bunche and the rejection of his son by a certain tennis club because of his color. No valid excuse could be made for the club committee, but furor raised by the N.A.A.C.P. was hardly worthy of approval.

The episode was used by our Communist enemies to promote ill will for us, the implication being that all Americans are prejudiced. This simply isn't true. Dr. Bunche is a great and gifted man. By his services in the United Nations he has probably done more to gain respect for his race than any organization set up for its advancement. It is a shame he and his family were embarrassed. But let us be honest and admit that many Negroes do not measure up to him—nor many whites, for that matter. Integration does not mean that the rest of us shall lose the right to choose our friends and associates, Negro or white. It does mean that no one shall be denied rights or freedoms because of color or any other group 'tag' that may be applied to him. It means equal opportunity for self-improvement, and equal responsibility.

The processes of American democracy are constantly evolving. They may be slow in correcting minor ills, they may seem to condone injustices for a time, but far more certainly than any other system they can prevent, and should prevent, the denial of human dignity and worth to any segment of our population. There may be difficulties, even steps backward; the imperfections of man are reflected in man's ordinances as well as his behavior. But we have the basics written down in our Declaration of Independence, our Constitution, our Bill of Rights—and if we defend these for everybody, we shall find ourselves growing in the right direction.

Most of us are taught the fundamentals of our form of government, so well described in Lincoln's words 'of the people, by the people and for the people.' But how many schools and colleges teach what underlies these fundamentals? As ex-President Herbert Hoover said in an address at Stanford University: "We need to remember that a concept of the dignity and worth of the individual is perhaps the most significant contribution of American civilization to human progress, and to rededicate ourselves to the difficult realization of that ideal throughout the world." And what is equally important, how often are we taught the obligation of the individual to his government, and to the concepts which permit it to function?

A few years ago some friends and I had the privilege of establishing at Stanford University, with the cooperation of its president, Dr. J. E. Wallace Sterling, a fund for a professorship in Humanistic Studies as a memorial to a great friend of all of us, Harry Camp, who devoted most of his life to humanity. Meant to promote the study of the concept of human dignity and worth, it is our hope that the project will encourage similar efforts in other institutions of learning, here and abroad.

There is a great deal to be done in this field, both in the study of the historical development of the concept and its current significances in human relations—including those of business, labor, law, politics, literature and philosophy—and in the teaching that will stem from study of the concept, teaching that in time will filter down to elementary levels, so that the youngest child may benefit.

It is my deepest hope that this little book may accelerate the

process. In my unacademic way, I have tried to present a survey,
a 'synopsis' of what I have learned and earnestly feel about the
problems we Americans face, together with some background and
suggested solutions. It is inadequate, I know, but perhaps it will
help.

I would like to stress a number of points that, it seems to me,
are of particular importance.

*   *   *

In our system, more than in others, most problems eventually
descend to the individual. Our destiny as a nation depends on us—
on you, on me. It depends on how we behave as citizens, on how
much we appreciate our freedoms and our rights, on how much we
know about our history, how much we know about the forces
opposing us, and how we safeguard what we have for ourselves
and others.

Prejudice, intolerance and hate can build up. Ignite the spark,
and a blaze of hate can envelop our nation. More than ever before
in our life as a people we need unity, the realization of our common
cause—and enough of personal sacrifice to win in that common
cause. We can only weaken ourselves by permitting the division
of Americans into classes, whether of race, of group, or of economic
strata.

This does not mean that we should not unite in a cause, for our
betterment in any way. But let us unite as individuals and hesitate
to classify ourselves. Let us recognize that group union does not
compel us to surrender individual rights, and that group strength
should be exercised in the interests of all, not only for those within
the group. The stronger we are, the greater our obligation.

Minorities create their own problems, frequently. When they insist
on congregating in certain districts in cities, they draw attention to
themselves as minorities and conflicts develop. It would be far better
if these people dispersed. There is room for them in this country, in
places where they can find productive employment. We need willing
hands—and opportunity is to be found everywhere.

America owes what it is today to enduring faith in freedom, justice
and equality of opportunity for all men. With education, particularly
for newcomers who bring defensive prejudices with them, we should
be able to absorb our minorities much more efficiently—and magnify
their productiveness. Let us remember that the idea of integration

applies not only to colored people but to every individual who becomes an American. This we must know, recognize and teach. Ours is a true People's Democracy, not the so-called 'democracy' of oppressed masses or classes.

We are involved in a struggle for survival with these false democracies. We can never afford to forget the essential differences between their system and ours. Theirs is a totalitarian system, by which an individual wishing to change his station in life or raise his standard of living can accomplish it only by strict conformity, even in his thinking. It is a collectivist system that enforces regimentation and complete subservience to the ruling class, with low standards for everyone else; it is a government of the rulers, by the rulers and for the rulers.

If we are to maintain our freedoms and win out against the Communist drive for world domination, we must check our own morals and attitudes at home. They are vital in the battle of ideologies. We are prone to forget one of our own best assets in the fight—tolerance. Unless we solve our problems of human relations, Communism can very well win out, with the uncommitted portions of the world watching our handling of people in our own midst, who depend on American principles for protection. World War II was set off by the failure of the German people to practice tolerance, and the failure of the Western world to foresee the inevitable result of a build-up of hatreds. Surely, with the advantages we have, we can halt strife amongst our nearly 180 millions, and start fighting *for* each other—a people's fight for people's rights in the war the Communists have launched against freedom.

Our system is essentially flexible. We have free elections in which the vote of the individual is kept secret, freedom to discuss and argue, freedom to compromise in public affairs, and absolute separation of the executive and judicial branches of government. With various local changes elements of our system have spread through many parts of the world, though we do not seek to impose it on anyone. At the same time we hold it dear, and believe that our institutions have made a very real contribution to the world.

But we must watch trends in our system which may destroy individual freedoms. Does a leader standing for election identify himself too closely with a 'class,' a group, an organization? We must be ever vigilant against leadership and government by any element in our society dedicated to its own interests. We must

beware of regimentation, jealously guard our rights to vote and think
as individuals.

At the moment, a crucial conflict is mounting between business
and labor. What is 'business' but a name signifying an association
of men supplying the brains to enhance our way of living? Labor
makes use of these brains, profits by them. If we as individuals
recognize that business and labor are one under our system, and
contribute our pressure to end senseless strife, we can halt our head-
long course towards inflation and disaster.

You and I are not working for 'big' business, 'big' labor or 'big'
government—we are working for the betterment of all. And it
wouldn't be a bad idea if we could bring home to these factions in
our culture that they are working for *us*.

If we permit division between business and labor, government is
bound to step in. And then what happens? Regulation, restriction
of freedoms, more and more 'statism'—and, in the end, Fascism or
some other kind of dictatorship, perhaps even Communism, with the
wielders of power arousing prejudice and intolerance, and encouraging
further divisions into groups and classes that form in sheer self-
defense.

This is a path too much of the world has followed. Fascism and
Nazism both developed out of class conflicts which bowed to the
dictators' formula of 'divide and rule.' Some may argue that it
can't happen here. But we are not living in normal times, and what
might emerge from a severe national crisis no one can foretell. I do
not believe that any of us would knowingly sacrifice this country
and its freedoms for his party, his business or his union. Far too
few of us, however, are alert to the need for national unity in the
war we wage with our ideological enemies.

It is brought home to you when you travel in foreign lands. Then
you realize that only those who have lost their freedoms understand
how precious they are, and how easily they may be lost. You know
it *can* happen in America, and it comes to you, with a chill in the
stomach, that there is a great need for review and reindoctrination
of the principles by which American liberties are sustained.

The insidious thing about Communist waging of the cold war,
the ideological war, is that their approach is much more subtle and
deceptive than the propaganda mouthings of Hitler, Mussolini and
their gangs. And we are much more vulnerable these days. America
is the leader of the free world.

Our incredibly high standard of living—incredible to the rest of the world—is used to arouse envy and dislike. They steal and twist our terms, such as 'democracy' and 'freedom,' to substantiate their Big Lie that we are 'imperialists' in their effort to disguise the fact that they are the real imperialists. Our freedoms of speech and of the press are used against us—their false charges are often printed in this country, with some effect, while anything we have to say is censored behind the Iron Curtain, or subverted to mean the opposite of what we mean.

Because of our freedoms, we live in a fish bowl; their schemes are locked in a safe. The sensationalism of a portion of our press only helps their cause. Their aim is to keep men's minds so stuffed with propaganda that the truth can never emerge. The distinction between lies and truth becomes ever more dim, in this word-war. Is it any wonder that the under-developed peoples of the world are confused? That they hesitate to follow our way to democracy?

We need to embark on an effective information campaign, world-wide, telling the simple, unadorned facts. We do not want dominions; we want friends, friends we will help as they help us. Perhaps we should invent new words to replace those the Communists have stolen. But the great fact we should emphasize is that Communism is unalterably opposed to independent thinking, to any effort of man to improve himself outside their corrosive system, and to any seeking of man for God, within his own mind and heart.

Indeed, Communism's principal enemy is religion—faith in anything except the tortuous Marxist-Leninist-Stalinist-Krushchev line threatens the very basis of the state religion Communism is trying to impose.

Totalitarian Communism is so far out of date that its fanatics are determined to ram it down the world throat in a manner not unlike that of the Moslem *jihad* of 1,000 years ago. Isn't it incredible that in this modern era, the twentieth century, another 'holy war' should have been launched, this time against all humanity? And, moreover, that the insane challenge is still the same—*believe or die?*

It is this aspect of Communism's atheistic crusade, I believe, which will bring about its eventual defeat. The opportunity to worship is individual man's deepest need, and the gods Communism provides are not worthy. They are human gods, with more than their share of human faults.

Perhaps our churches, by uniting in brotherhood and in tolerance of each other, down to the last individual member of any congregation, can bring home to us, as individuals, a renewed sense of man's destiny—to aspire to God's perfection and teach the dangers of hate as well as the gospel of love.

With this ideal, perhaps we can all of us so behave that we do not act in a manner inimical to the destiny and security of our country, the United States of America.

XI

THE OUTLOOK

In sober appraisal of the future, I must say that never before—speaking from my knowledge and experience—has it looked so uncertain for America and Americans.

Of course, not everyone agrees with me. In December 1959, for instance, *Life* magazine came out with its annual special issue, entitled *The Good Life*, in which thousands of words and several hundred photos were devoted to detailing the luxuries and leisure delights in store for us over the next decade or so. A few conservative notes were sounded. The most significant was a somewhat casual remark to the effect that the 'good life' so copiously illustrated depended on the possibility of obtaining a period of peace.

It is to be devoutly hoped that we do. And it may be that an accommodation for the lessening of tensions between East and West can be reached. But so far we have had little real assurance of it, and we would be the wildest of optimists if we counted on it. All evidence from the past would indicate that we are not yet out of trouble. We shall be wiser if we count on *that*.

To me it isn't merely a question of trouble, but the degree of trouble we encounter. If we can reduce the costs and anxieties of the cold war we shall be lucky; we are more apt, in the long run, to find it continuing more or less as at present. If it goes badly for us, an economic crisis more severe than any in our history may come upon us. At worst, we can meet with military catastrophe.

So far as the cold war situation is concerned, let us not forget that the gravest threat to our internal security is inflation—and we now seem to be in for another round of it, as usual stemming from the settlement of a steel strike even if union gains were not as great as formerly. Whether this round can become the critical one, no one knows as yet.

But it isn't going to do us any good. Once more the dollar declines in value, everything costs more, the government edges more deeply into deficit financing, interest rates go up, people's savings are worth less, our foreign trade suffers, and other countries are increasingly wary of our currency.

From the shortsighted, probably, an outcry will once more come for inflationary government measures to ease the mounting cost of borrowing, begetting more inflation. If we, the people, permit this, the balloon may not burst tomorrow, but when it does we shall have that economic crisis I mentioned—and we will have lost the cold war to the Communists, our strength vitiated.

In that case, it will probably not be necessary for them to launch a hot war.

Another threat to our security, scarcely less grave, is that posed by the conspiratorial Communist Party in our own midst. For forty years these zealots have plotted for a Soviet America in the service of the Kremlin. If you doubt that this is serious, read J. Edgar Hoover's book, *Masters Of Deceit.* Almost from the beginning that staunch American and the F.B.I. have been fighting the Party here, and he should know whether our domestic traitors are dangerous.

True, C.P.U.S.A. membership—the known membership, that is— has declined to around 20,000 of recent years. But these are largely hard-core revolutionists in the Lenin mold, and there are probably at least that many more underground and strategically located as 'sleepers' in our industry. In time of stress these saboteurs, together with actual Soviet agents in the networks operating within our borders, could wreak incalculable damage, perhaps cripple American production.

Of course, the Party's ultimate aim is revolution. They may be optimistic in thinking they can achieve it. But what do they plan for us, if they are right? Quoting Mr. Hoover:

"All industry would be nationalized and farms taken away from their owners. A small businessman is just as guilty as a large businessman; both must be liquidated. Rents, profits and insurance would be abolished. Countless occupations, termed by the Communists as 'useless and parasitic,' would be ended. Here is a part of their list: wholesalers, jobbers, real estate men and stockbrokers, advertising specialists, traveling salesmen, lawyers, 'whole rafts of government bureaucrats, police, clericals, and sundry capitalist quacks, fakers and grafters.' The Communists have a special disdain for lawyers. Perhaps it is because there will be no need for lawyers when there are no rights to defend. . . .

"Action would be drastic, immediate, and without appeal. An armed 'Red Guard' would enforce the orders of Party henchmen. Hotels, country clubs, and swimming pools would be used for the benefit of 'workers,' meaning, in most cases, Party bosses. The workingman in the mines, factories, and mills would be told to work certain hours for certain wages. Labor unions, as we know them, would be obliterated. All such organizations would be controlled and operated by the Communist government; no laborer would be permitted to organize a union or to strike against his 'government.'

"The press would be muzzled, free speech forbidden, and complete conformity demanded. If you expressed an opinion contrary to the Party line, you should have known better and your 'disappearance' would serve as a lesson for others. Fear becomes an enforcement technique. Movies, radio and television would be taken over by the government as agencies for government propaganda. Churches would probably not be closed immediately, but they would be heavily taxed, their property seized by the state, and religious schools liquidated. Clergymen would be required to accept the Party line. 'God does not exist. Why worship Him?' say the Communists. Children would be placed in nurseries and special indoctrination schools. Women, boast the Communists, would be relieved of housework. How? Huge factory and apartment-house kitchens would be set up, so that women would be 'free' to work in factories and mines along with the men. . . .

" . . . Communists want to control everything: where you live, where you work, what you are paid, what you think, what street-cars you ride (or whether you walk), how your children are educated, what you may not and must read and write. The most minute details, even the time your alarm clock goes off in the morning or the amount of cream in your coffee are subjects for state supervision. They want to make a 'Communist man,' a mechanical puppet, whom they can train to do as the Party desires. This is the ultimate, and tragic, aim of Communism."

And that is the way of life that has been forced on about one billion individuals in Russia, China and the Iron Curtain countries. I suppose our own Communists feel that what is good enough for others is good enough for us.

Why haven't these internal enemies of ours been suppressed? They are protected by our own laws, plus certain rulings of the Supreme Court, of which they take full advantage. Surely it is time we did something to protect ourselves more adequately. While it may be that Red revolution 'can't' happen here, 'isn't it ridiculous to take the chance.

Remember, the Russian people didn't want Bolshevik rule, but they fell to a disciplined minority—and our Communists have the might of two huge Red nations behind them.

In our world relations we can naturally expect our most serious trouble from the U.S.S.R., and from Communist China. At the very least, I feel, the cold war will continue until the mental illness of Communism begins to fade into history—possibly after another ten years, more likely twenty years, perhaps longer. Our main hope is to wear the enemy out, prove him wrong by continuing to demonstrate the superiority of Western civilizations, and wait for disillusionment to set in when the present Red leaders are no longer gods, but dead men.

Honest competition could be healthy. In fact, we'd win that much sooner if there were any honesty at all in Communism. But the Red goal of world dominion, which can only be looked on as criminal by free men and free nations, has not been abandoned—and it won't be until it becomes plainly impossible to the Reds themselves. Meanwhile, we can anticipate every sort of international skulduggery and double-dealing, despite Mr. Khrushchev's waving of the olive branch.

If any concrete evidence of good faith should emerge in his proposals—and it appears that he really speaks for the entire Red regime—well and good. We could begin to build a more cordial relationship, while continuing to be wary. But it is more than probable that his peace overtures are a maneuver to split the nations of the West.

The reaction of our NATO allies is a little disheartening. With an estimated one hundred missile-launching positions established in Russia, most of them aimed at Europe, they are still eager to respond to the slightest sign of Soviet softening. They're afraid, naturally; but we have just as much to fear in this day of the long-range ICBM. So does Russia, for that matter. But Khrushchev, a dictator, can make more effective use of threats, and he shrewdly presses his advantage.

What could please him most of all, perhaps, would be to get us involved in a war with China on India's side. We could whittle down China's strength and exhaust our own, especially if our European friends stood aside or took little part, while Russia gave China only enough aid to keep her in the battle. Such a situation has its precedent in Korea. And this is the strategy we could have used to great profit with Russia and Germany in World War II. Only this time we would be in Russia's role, fighting our way to oblivion.

The whole thing could be set up as a 'local' war, with atomic weapons barred. If we used them on China, or attacked Russia, the world could explode. It is not pleasant to contemplate—and it might well be what Khrushchev has in mind.

Thus, a possibility for military disaster. . . .

We know from history that the light of liberty will never diminish, and that man is inalienably free even when born in shackles, and that a free world must emerge as one world eventually. But in our time, the question is not resolved.

A dark age of Communist oppression can descend, and the dream of One World, free for all mankind, can be frustrated for generations of man to come.

What can we do—you and I?

We can remember that leadership is not the prerogative of one man or even of a group of men—it is something that must be exercised in basic ways by a people, through a system in which they believe, and value. We have such a system, and plentiful reason to value it.

We can demonstrate to other peoples of the world, those of newly developing nations in particular, that their aspirations can best be met in a free society. We cannot be found wanting in the supreme test of our free and democratic way of life that now faces us.

Missiles alone won't save us. We need 'heads' as well as 'arms.' It is not a question of electing one man to represent us, although we need a dynamic leader who must command the respect and confidence of our people. It is not a question of electing politicians to serve in our legislatures and other public offices—and then turning to our pleasures until election time rolls around again. It is not a question of depending on political parties to preserve our interests.

It is a question of issues. We need not agree on all, but we must agree on one—our leadership as a people, a people dedicated to world liberty, knowing that our liberty, our freedoms, must be extended to others in whatever degrees the rest of mankind is ready for them.

Until recent years, there has been no dire need for the kind of popular leadership that only the American people can exert. Often the world has misunderstood discordancies in our politics; other peoples do not appreciate how united we really are. Let us emphasize our unity in our communications, in our arts, in our individual contacts with people abroad. And let us strive for more unity, through understanding, among still divided groups in our own social commonalty.

Never in history has another nation possessed anything to equal the great gifts of our American heritage.

It is up to us—the American people—to make sure the next generations choose wisely between the Totalitarian Idea, that malign force that masquerades as democracy today, and the genuine Democratic Idea, which has been growing, and shall grow, until all men realize their ultimate destiny in freedom.

*   *   *

It is claimed our prestige is down these days; if so, it is because we have not kept our chins up. Not necessarily our leaders but the American public must accept some blame. Prestige is not wealth, power and force. Russia, with all three can lay no claims to prestige. Prestige is the force which is attained by high achievement—for a person or a country to be admired for its or his strength of character, its integrity and the respect generated by its basic principles and beliefs based on truth and honest endeavors.

Our new President represents a new voice of America, a young voice which will take its place in new world opinion. He has the position to do so and he has the vitality and the youth to lead the world in a new philosophy of right as well as might. He is a man of great courage. He must now state our position clearly, as a free country. As long as prosperity and security seemed assured it did not seem necessary to restate the meanings of freedom. He must make the American people understand, and the world understand, we are determined to defend our underlying principles under any circumstances and to impress the world with that determination.

It is essential to develop, at home, a responsible, interested public, ready to make sacrifices to retain their freedom and to become partners and not just spectators. It is important to change the image of our might, if necessary, the image of man dedicated to remain free and ready to fight for that cause when our shores are in danger. President Kennedy must make it clear we intend to enforce the Monroe Doctrine at all costs, to protect our nationalism as others would protect theirs.

Nationalism must start with a code of ethics. It can never last when established through theft and plunder of other peoples property, whose investments were encouraged by foreign lands which welcomed such aid. We must demand respect for the rights of American citizens and refuse to recognize brigandry. We must insist that only by recognizing the rights of others can one's own right be protected.

Our President must tell the world that we are also a young nation, that we intend to fully protect our interests, that our investments abroad must be respected, and that we will not permit pillage and theft as the basis for a new freedom.

New nations need foreign investments; they have needed them in the past and should encourage them for their future. They and their leaders are responsible for their own peace and the peace of the world; they must not be permitted to play with stacked cards. Some seem to believe that Communism and democracy can be played, one against the other, for self interest and selfish personal motives. They forget that America won its freedom by its contribution to the forces which recognized the advancement of the human being, and that even Russia and the United States might find a common denominator, a middle road for the sake of man's survival.

Our tomorrow can be blessed with a new movement to counteract the teachings of hate and greed which were let loose by Nazism. Our President can create the image of young America. He can lead a world youth movement for truth and honesty. He can stress good relations, not poor relations. He can promote human relations and good will. He can insist we will be tough with enemies and helpful to friends. He can stay at home and issue cordial invitations for others to visit us. With these basic principles, he should alert the Western nations that they must not permit themselves to become bullied and cynical. We are ready for a revitalization of American initiative, humanity, and realism.